Imitation and Education

SUNY series, The Philosophy of Education

Philip L. Smith, editor

Imitation and Education

A Philosophical Inquiry into Learning by Example

BRYAN R. WARNICK

State University of New York Press

Published by
State University of New York Press, Albany

For information, contact State University of New York Press, Albany, NY
www.sunypress.edu

Production by Ryan Morris
Marketing by Michael Campochiaro

Library of Congress Cataloging-in-Publication Data

Warnick, Bryan R., 1974–
   Imitation and education : a philosophical inquiry into learning by
example / Bryan R. Warnick.
        p. cm. — (SUNY series, the philosophy of education)
   Includes bibiographical references and index.
   ISBN: 978-0-7914-7427-3 (hardcover : alk. paper)
   1. Education—Philosophy.   2. Example.   3. Imitation.   4. Learning,
Psychology of.   I. Title.

LB14.7.W375 2008
370.1—dc22   2007024952

10 9 8 7 6 5 4 3 2 1

To Elizabeth

caret initio et fine

Contents

Acknowledgments   ix

Chapter 1   The Problems of Imitation and Human Exemplarity   1
   Introduction   1
   The Mysteries of Learning by Example: An Outline   9

Chapter 2   The Historical Tradition of Human Exemplarity   13
   Imitative Models of Human Exemplarity: The Standard Model   13
   Enlightenment Criticism and Nonimitative Exemplars   18
   The Historical Tradition: An Initial Assessment   26

Chapter 3   How Do People Become Examples?   31
   The Nature of Examples   33
   How Does Something Become an Example?   37
   Educational Implications   44
   Conclusion   49

Chapter 4   How Do Examples Bring Out Imitation?   53
   The Link between Action and Perception   57
   The Sense of Self and the Imitative Sorting Mechanism   61
   The Narrative-Self Theory of Imitation   65
   The Social Nature of Narrative and Imitation   73
   Educational Implications   77
   Conclusion   82

Chapter 5   The Social Meanings of Imitation   83
   The Meanings of Following an Example   87
   Imitation and Community Identity   93
   Imitation, Initiation, and Education   97
   Factors Influencing Imitative Meaning   100
   Imitation and Communities of Learning   105
   Conclusion   107

Chapter 6   Imitation, Exemplarity, and Moral Reason   109
    The Practical Objection to Imitating Examples   110
    A Social Response to the Practical Objection   113
    The Theoretical Objection to Imitating Examples   119
    A Social Response to the Theoretical Objection   120
    Conclusion   125

Chapter 7   How Can We Evaluate Human Exemplars?   127
    Ancient Skepticism, Exemplarity, and Criticality   129
    The Turn to Practices and Exemplar Rotation   134
    A Critical Education and Exemplarity: A Conclusion   136

Chapter 8   A Social Analysis of Exemplarity and Imitation   139

Notes   147

References   153

Index   163

Acknowledgments

Several people deserve recognition for their help with this project. Nicholas Burbules, Walter Feinberg, Pradeep Dhillon, and Stephen Jaeger at the University of Illinois all read this manuscript and offered substantive and challenging feedback. Nick, in particular, has been and continues to be an encouraging teacher, even now that I have moved on from his official domain of responsibility. Phil Smith has proven to be equally supportive in my new position at The Ohio State University.

My initial thinking about this project began at the Stanford–Illinois Summer Institute for Philosophy of Education, held in Palo Alto, California, in 2003. The faculty and students with whom I discussed my fledgling ideas gave me the needed confidence to start developing this book. The institute was a memorable gift made possible by funding from the Spencer Foundation.

More distant in space and time from the writing of this book, but equally important were family and friends. My parents have been supportive at every critical juncture of my life and they form the foundational exemplars that I would hope to imitate. Finally, I owe a huge debt of gratitude to my wife Ellie and my children, Nora and Andrew.

Portions of this book have been adapted from Bryan Warnick, "How Do We Learn from the Lives of Others?" In *Philosophy of Education 2006,* ed. Daniel Vokey (Urbana, Illinois: Philosophy of Education Society, 2007), 367–75. Reprinted by permission of the Philosophy of Education Society.

CHAPTER 1

The Problems of Imitation and Human Exemplarity

The Great Man was always as lightning out of Heaven; the rest of men waited for him like fuel, and then they too would flame.

—Thomas Carlyle, *On Heroes,
Hero Worship, and the Heroic in History*

INTRODUCTION

My life has been a mirror of the lives lived around me. I find myself becoming like the people I am exposed to; I reproduce their actions and attitudes. Only rarely, however, can I recall making a conscious decision to imitate. One of my teachers was such a towering personality that he radically changed the direction of my life, though I was scarcely aware of his influence at the time. Only long after did I recognize his imprimatur emerging on everything from my occupational decisions, to my views about religion and politics, and even to my preferences about where to go for lunch. I seem to have been passive fuel awaiting his incendiary presence. When I think about his influence, I wonder how it occurred and whether it has, on the whole, been a good thing for me to have learned in this imitative way. This book is, among other things, a personal attempt to answer questions about how I became who I am. It is an attempt to understand

*nice
prose*

1

how one human life can sway another and to better comprehend the meaning and value of this influence.

These questions, of course, are far from being of merely personal interest. The topic of imitative learning and human exemplarity is often present in discussions of human development in local and national communities, in scholarly circles, and in the mass media. People usually discuss the topic using the phrase "role models," a term that is somehow intended to cover a wide variety of learning processes. Consider how often the language of role modeling arises in educational discourse. Conservatives place role models as central features in character education programs. Liberals, in turn, view the absence of role models for minority students as a major justification for affirmative action initiatives. Christian children are urged to do what Jesus would do, which is merely one manifestation of the tradition of *imitatio dei* shared by many world religions. Endless debate surrounds the status and value of celebrities and athletes as role models, while new teachers are urged to find and imitate experienced mentors during their first years of employment. Learning technologies are designed to help students imitate experts within particular domains of scientific practice. Clearly, the notions of modeling, imitation, and exemplarity are some of the central concepts in contemporary educational and social discourse.

Looking at the history of Western educational thought, one finds a similar emphasis on exemplars and imitation. The topic is emphasized by Platonists and Sophists, Skeptics and Stoics, poets and monks, Christians and Jews. Human exemplars have been given a privileged place in the educational thought of philosophers as different as Locke, Nietzsche, Aristotle, Rousseau, and Wittgenstein. Some have celebrated imitative learning, others have condemned it, but few have ignored it.

And yet, what have contemporary philosophers and educational theorists had to say about this topic? Not as much as one would think. In spite of their prominence in contemporary social discourse, questions of human exemplarity, modeling, and imitation have been largely ignored. Although flashes of insight sporadically appear, human exemplarity and imitation have not been the subjects of extended philosophical discussion and reflection. This neglect has left the continuous contemporary stream of assertions about human exemplars lacking a vitality and richness. We are left with little understanding of how one life shapes another.

This neglect may have arisen because questions about human exemplarity can quickly reduce to empirical questions and are thus considered the domain of psychologists or sociologists—after all, phi-

quote for modeling article

losophers often cannot or do not want to enter the messy world of empirical claims and counterclaims. The neglect may also have occurred because there seems to be little philosophical mystery involved with learning through human exemplars: We see somebody being successful, we observe the action closely, and then we attempt to replicate the actions we observe. At times it appears there is little more to do than to advocate this process as an educational truism, or warn against it, perhaps, if we do not like the idea of imitating others.

Under the apparent simplicity of human exemplarity and imitation, however, remain many unanswered questions. Indeed, the process by which human exemplars work their influence appears particularly mysterious. My own experience has told me that I usually do not choose to imitate my exemplars; it is more that the exemplars somehow choose me. The apparent clarity of human exemplarity often appears to be nothing more than the façade of a building occupied with theoretical obscurity. Contemporary discussions of role models, it sometimes seems, presume to know the answers to questions we still do not even know how to ask.

To illustrate the mystery involved with human exemplarity, one can turn to the field of medical education. In one study of medical schools (Wright, S.M., et al., 1998), students were surveyed to find out who functioned as their professional role models and exemplars. Students generally responded by saying that doctors who displayed enthusiasm, compassion, openness, integrity, and caring relationships with patients were their models (I will label these physicians as "people-oriented" physicians). When anthropologists observe the actual practices of medical students, however, there appears a gap between who students claim to hold as models and who the students actually appear to imitate. Instead of imitating the favorable traits of compassion and openness, students instead focus on "status-oriented" values. Paice, Heard, and Moss discuss the work of Simon Sinclair and worry about his finding that students imitate physicians who have responsibility, power, and prestige. The students, they find, were "not impressed by doctors who seemed to share their power and responsibility with other professionals." They continue: "These observations suggest a divergence between the qualities that students and young doctors say they seek in their role models and the qualities that they actually emulate" (2002, p. 708). Indeed, if the students are honestly responding to the questions of the role model survey (and we have no reason to think they are not), and if they really do fail to take the people-oriented type of physicians as models, then something seems amiss. What explains this mismatch between who students think of as their models and who they actually imitate? If the students are not intentionally choosing the examples to imitate, how are the examples selected?

These are not idle questions. The mystery of exemplars and their educational influence has important implications for public policy. One of the most contested areas of policy relates to concerns about media violence and how children might imitate the mayhem they are exposed to in films, television, or video games. Such worries are justified. There is, in fact, a well documented correlation between exposure to violent media and the performance of violent episodes later in life (Anderson & Bushman, 2002; Bushman & Anderson, 2001; Johnson, Cohen, Smailes, Kasen, & Brook, 2002; Wilson & Wilson, 1998). There may even be a documented causal connection between the two (Huesmann et al., 2003). The relationship, however, must surely be complex. After all, most people who are exposed to violence do not reenact or imitate the *specific* sort of violence they see. Copycat violence does happen, of course, but it usually occurs in only a tiny fraction of people exposed to a specific representation of violence. Millions of people heard about Robert Speck's murder of eight nurses in 1966, but the incident only spawned one known imitator. Other violent acts, however, seem to have a greater imitative salience, and it is not entirely clear why this would be so. The school shootings at Columbine High School in 1999 produced 20 known imitators—still only a tiny fraction of people imitated the violence, to be sure, but this crime seemed to fire the imitative imagination more than the Speck murders. There are also questions about the specific sorts of violent representations that spawn imitative violence. Is it more than just the usual suspects of movies and video games? What about the depictions of war or murder in the newspaper or television news? What about reading or watching the bloody scenes in a Shakespearean play? And what about those people who report that, after viewing a violent film, they have become even more nonviolent than before? In such cases the violent depictions appear to be taken as negative examples (the examples are repulsive) and this suggests that simply viewing media violence by itself does not seem to be enough to trigger imitation. There is a need, then, to better understand the process by which we are influenced by observing other human lives.

Fortunately, many recent studies allow us to gain a fuller understanding of exemplarity, imitation, and education. There has been an explosion of research in cognitive science on the topic of imitation, with several major research compilations published only recently (Dautenhahn & Nehaniv, 2002a; Hurley & Chater, 2005a; Meltzoff & Prinz, 2002). Philosophers, especially those concerned with human development and education, have not paid enough attention to these

no Bandura ?!

new research developments. In an introduction to their volume on imitation, Susan Hurley and Nick Chater correctly assert that the new research on imitation has "yet to be assimilated" in social science and philosophy, even as it has become a topic of "intense current interest in the cognitive sciences" (2005b, p. 1).

This lack of interest is unfortunate because there are many ways in which philosophers can benefit from engaging with this research, as well as many ways in which they can contribute to a better understanding of human exemplarity and imitation. They can contribute by doing the obvious things that philosophers do. For example, they can specify the assumptions made in discussions of role models and imitative learning, and they can also work to assess the meaning, value, and genuine limitations of imitative learning. In addition, a little imagination reveals other possibilities of philosophical contribution. Philosophers, after all, have been actively working in the field of exemplarity for the past several decades. Nelson Goodman's work in the 1970s introduced a flurry of interest in the topic among Anglo-American philosophers. More recently, philosopher Irene Harvey (2002) has published a book that claims on the cover to be "the first, comprehensive, in-depth study of the problem of exemplarity." Harvey examines exemplarity from the perspective of continental philosophy and utilizes theorists such as Rousseau and Derrida. Thus, there is a continuing interest in exemplarity in both analytic and continental philosophy. It is possible that this research can contribute to the discussion about the framing of models and the production of imitative responses in a way that has been largely missing from the empirical literature on imitation. What I intend to do, therefore, is to examine these disconnected literatures on imitation and exemplarity, put them together where possible, and apply them in thinking about education and social policy.

Before proceeding, let me attempt to clarify some possible conceptual confusion. In this study, I will be using the terms human "example," "model," and "exemplar" interchangeably. These terms are, to be sure, slightly different. An exemplar or model is one type of human example that has achieved a kind of normative force. It is a specific manifestation of the more general idea of an example, much like a "car" is a specific manifestation of a "vehicle." These differences, however, will usually be irrelevant for my purposes, and I will vary my vocabulary for stylistic purposes (just as one might want to legitimately vary the use of "car" and "vehicle").

I will use the term "imitation" in its broad sense. Various distinctions have been proposed relating to the concepts of "imitation," "emulation," and "mimicry." These distinctions are often built around a

Terms

framework of means and ends. In its more technical sense, "imitation" has come to mean reproducing a model's action in a way that aims at the same goal as the model. That is to say, true imitation is an action that replicates both the means and ends of the model's action. The action, it is also stipulated, must be novel—that is, a true imitation must be an action that the imitator has never done before. In contrast, "emulation" is said to occur when an observer attempts to attain the same ends as a model through different means, while "mimicry" takes place when an observer reproduces the means of action without sharing the model's ends. In addition, there are also technical labels for behaviors that appear to reproduce the actions of a model but that fail to participate in any framework of means and ends. For example, "stimulus enhancement" is said to occur when a model's behavior calls an observer's attention to an object of interest, while "response priming" is said to occur with the transmission of simple behavioral reflexes—think of contagious yawning. These processes give rise to behaviors that often look like imitation, but do not involve reproducing the means or ends of intentional action.

Generally speaking, I will not use these technical distinctions, largely because I have doubts about our ability to adequately differentiate means and ends in action—an ability that all these distinctions seem to require. What appears to be emulating an end or goal from one perspective (becoming a millionaire, just like a rich uncle) may also be a further means to something else (living a happy life, just like the rich uncle). In real life, ends in one framework are usually themselves means to further ends. Another problem has to do with imitative actions that are goal driven but occur even though the imitator does not share the same goals of the model (an imitator may, in fact, not even know the goals of the model). Consider a person who imitates members of a group, not to accomplish the group's goals but to fit in socially with members of the group. This is surely not simple mimicry, but it does not fit the technical definition of imitation either. For these reasons and others, I will use the term "imitation" to designate an action that reproduces the behaviors, attitudes, or lifestyles of another person and that is, furthermore, instigated by the idea or perception of that person's behaviors, attitudes, or lifestyles (rather than being instigated, say, by the presence of a rule saying that everybody should act in similar ways). Thus, I will be using "imitation" in its broad sense rather than in its technical sense.

Some may wonder why the concepts of imitation and exemplarity should be brought together in this study. It is true that the topics are, in many ways, distinct. But there are rich and complex relationships between the concepts of "being an example" and "imitation." Consider two questions that can be raised about the relationship between these concepts: First, if we say that somebody is serving as an example, do we imply that the person is necessarily being imitated? Second, if we say somebody is being imitated, is that person then necessarily serving as an example of something? With regard to the first question, it appears that most people do sense a conceptual relationship between being an example and being imitated. We often use such phrases as "following Jones's example" when discussing imitative action. Not all examples of human life, however, are linked to imitation in ordinary discourse. Some examples are offered precisely because they are not to be imitated ("Jones is an example of what not to do"). This implies that not all examples of human life that influence human development do so by bringing out an imitative response, at least not in any obvious way. Thus, examples are often, but not always, linked to imitative actions. Although this book will discuss several forms of human exemplarity, even educational examples that are not imitated, those examples that do provoke imitation will be the central focus.

The second question does not ask whether exemplarity is always linked to imitation, but asks instead if imitation is always linked to exemplarity. That is, when we imitate people, do we always imitate their *example*? Answering this question will require a look at the nature of exemplarity (and of imitation, for that matter) and this will be the topic of subsequent chapters. On a superficial level, at least, we could say that imitation of human beings is always of a particular slice of the category of human beings. If by an "example" we mean any particular sample of a larger whole, then we almost always seem to imitate an example. That is, we usually do not imitate "human beings" in general.

On a deeper level we could say that imitation involves a conceptualization of the nature and goals of the observed action. It involves a categorization of what the observed action is, exactly, and this process of categorizing specific instances under general groupings is what it means to think of something as an example. This categorization is even linked to perceptual issues and plays a part in determining what we see. The processes of perception, in other words, seem to be closely related to exemplification. When we see a person doing something and ask what the person is doing, we can always place the action under many different sorts of categories. If I were somehow to watch Gavrilo Princip shooting the Archduke Franz Ferdinand in 1914, I might perceive the action in different ways.

I might see that action as moving the index finger, or pulling a trigger, or shooting a human being, or committing a crime, or assassinating a political figure, or striking a blow for Serbian nationalism, or starting World War I. This seemingly endless expansion of possible descriptions of an action has been called the "accordion effect" in philosophy. The action can be accurately conceptualized in all these different ways and probably many others.

In the process of observing any action we invoke categories to help us determine what we see. To see how perception is influenced by conceptualization, think of the famously ambiguous duck-rabbit drawings (Fig. 1.1). Whether we perceive a duck or rabbit is a product of how we are paying attention to the figure, and our attention is focused by our conceptual knowledge and expectations. This process of categorizing the particular thing we see into a more general group is the process of exemplification—moving from the general to the particular and from the particular to the general. When working with the concept of a duck, we look for those characteristics that exemplify a duck. When we want to see a rabbit, we do the same thing. The concept we "have in mind" changes what we see.

When we see an action, it is exemplification (or a process like exemplification) that governs how we conceptualize action. Exemplification could be said to determine what we see the action *as*. The

emp support ?!

Figure 1.1. Ambiguous drawing by Joseph Jastrow (1899)

same holds true for other forms of perception besides vision. A Japanese speaker hears something different when Japanese is spoken than I do as a non-Japanese speaker, even though our eardrums are presumably all vibrating in similar ways. I hear the noises as structured unintelligible language (not gibberish, certainly, but still something incomprehensible). A native Japanese speaker, on the other hand, may hear an example of traditional Japanese poetry. Such obvious phenomena strongly suggest that perception is mediated by our conceptual understandings, and the process by which larger concepts subsume the particulars we encounter in experience is a process aligned with exemplification.

What this means is that the category of action that we draw from observing a model will influence the nature of the imitation that is produced, and this suggests a deep connection between imitation and exemplification. An imitative action we produce in response to Gavrilo Princip will depend on what, exactly, we "see" him doing—is he, for instance, an example of shooting a firearm or of engaging in political action? The first conceptualization might find me harmlessly imitating by sport shooting, the second by working for a political campaign. Both actions are legitimate imitations, but they are based on vastly different exemplifications. In short, what we imitate depends on the type of action that we perceive. In response to the question of whether all imitation is of examples, then, the proper response seems to be yes: Imitation always depends on exemplifications of actions. Given these connections between imitation and exemplification, philosophers who have discussed exemplification have much to contribute. This literature on "seeing as examples" is a missing piece in the cognitive science discussions of imitation.

THE MYSTERIES OF LEARNING BY EXAMPLE: AN OUTLINE

Besides connecting imitation with exemplarity, the initial contribution of philosophy comes through the traditional task of uncovering hidden assumptions; in this case, the assumptions that are implicit in the discourse surrounding modeling, imitation, and education. Contemporary discussions have doubtless been burdened with the presuppositions inherited from previous ages. To set up the important questions, then, I examine the assigned roles of imitative learning and human exemplarity in the historical tradition of educational thought. This investigation begins in chapter 2 with an analysis of how the discourse surrounding human exemplars has developed over time. By looking at selections of educational writings from Homer to Nietzsche, I trace how positions on human exemplarity have evolved in the Western tradition and I assess the tradition's overall merits and limitations.

The great strength of the Western tradition is that it proposes many possible roles for human exemplars in education; it reveals, in other words, the scope of possibilities. While the sheer variety of proposals about the place of exemplars in human learning is an important achievement, to be sure, the survey of the educational tradition also brings out the significant and questionable assumptions that continue to influence contemporary discourse. These assumptions relate to mysteries involving (a) the process of example selection, (b) the development of imitative motivation, and (c) the nature of human reason as it relates to imitative action. Once these three assumptions are revealed, the next chapters analyze each of these assumptions with the help of groups of literature from philosophy, psychology, and cognitive science. One of the goals of this book is to place groups of heretofore disconnected literatures together to see if they address the problematic assumptions of the traditional discourse surrounding imitation and human examples.

In chapter 3, I explore the first questionable assumption in the discourse surrounding human exemplarity; namely, the question of what an example is and how an example is selected. Examples not only seem to possess certain features, but they must communicate those features as well. In other words, an example must be a "telling" embodiment of a trait or quality. But how, exactly, does something become such a telling embodiment? In response to this question, I describe two processes by which this communicative aspect of examples is created. These processes of exemplarity demonstrate that examples are rooted in the concrete practices of particular communities and are dependent on structures of similarity and difference within social contexts. Human examples are not created through a simple interaction between the intentions of a teacher and the raw attributes of a model. Examples live, work, and have their being only insofar as they exist within certain social structures. This has important implications for education institutions, teaching practices, and the questions of media violence.

Chapter 4 analyzes the assumptions of the historical tradition by focusing on the mystery of how exemplars produce an imitative response. The chapter focuses on the assumptions revealed in the historical survey about how we become motivated to imitate examples. This question is essential because, while we must acknowledge that imitation is almost always a part of social interaction, it is clear that

Bandura

not every positive example of human life triggers a repetition. I may happily admit that Albert Einstein had an exemplary mind that I admire, but I do not find myself imitating him. I may be exposed to images of violence, but not act on them, or I may see them as examples of what not to do. Why do some examples bring out imitation while others do not? The chapter attempts to grapple with precisely this question and aims at constructing a more satisfying theory of how imitative action is produced or motivated.

The fifth chapter initiates a consideration of the assumptions about the relationship between imitation and human reason—a task that continues in the next two chapters. Chapter 5 also begins an examination of the value of imitative action and continues the task of applying relevant literatures in examining problematic assumptions of the discourse. One of the first steps in assessing the place of imitation in human reason and the value of imitation is grasping the meanings that imitative actions can bring to a social situation. The practices of "being an example" and "following an example," after all, have meaning in social contexts. Imitation can be, among other things, a sign of flattery, mockery, humility, worship, or dependency. In short, imitation can be a language that shapes and reshapes communities. Once we recognize that imitation has social meaning, perhaps the most intriguing mystery that arises is what imitation has to do with forming communities of practice and inquiry, or in other words, with forming educational communities.

The development of these social meanings of imitation continues to play a central role in chapter 6, where the discussion turns to questions dealing directly with the value of imitation and learning by example. In these sections, I enter the debate surrounding the contested place and prominence of human examples in moral education. Critics have argued that imitative action contradicts autonomous human reason and also that learning by imitation is unsuited to a world of rapid change and development. Although learning by example may have worked well in more stable societies, learners in today's world need to be able to "think for themselves"—that is, they should think creatively and produce independently justifiable reasons for their actions. Learning by example should therefore be deemphasized, some say, and a more rational, philosophic education should be put in its place. Against those who argue for this view, however, I will offer several arguments relating to the place of examples in human reason. Many of these arguments are based on the more social understanding of exemplarity and imitation developed in the previous chapters. Each argument attempts to undermine the alleged dichotomy between learning by imitation and a philosophic type of education where people "think for themselves." The purpose of this discussion is to begin to reconcile the value of imitative learning with the demands of critical reason.

The seventh chapter continues the discussions of criticality and imitation, but focuses specifically on the mystery of how we can think critically, not only in a general way, but specifically about the exemplars themselves. It is difficult to step outside of the influences of human examples. Even when we want to think critically about our examples, it seems that exemplarity constructs at least a part of our knowledge of what it means to do critical thinking. Since it is difficult to step outside of exemplarity, and since exemplarity is driven by social forces beyond our control, it is unclear how we might engage in an intelligent way with our normative models. Using the ancient Pyrrhonian Skeptics, however, I argue that an intelligent engagement with exemplars is possible, but it is a particular sort of engagement. I present one strategy for thinking about a difficult problem: How can we critically examine our examples, while not pretending to somehow remove ourselves from the influence of examples?

The last chapter highlights the central goal of this book: creating a better understanding of human exemplarity that will be useful in educational theory, educational practice, and larger social policy. My aim in gaining this understanding is not necessarily to argue for a greater emphasis on exemplars in educational institutions—indeed, current discussion surrounding role models suggests that the idea of learning from examples is hardly lacking in proponents. Rather than simply cheerleading for more use of role models in education (whatever that would mean), we would be better served by a more sophisticated theoretical discussion of how we are actually influenced by human lives and the value that we should attach to this influence. Assumptions about the functioning of human exemplarity exist in many different areas of educational thought, and, to put it bluntly, many of these assumptions are either wrong or underdeveloped. This is something that must change. Change must first begin by looking backward, though, and examining in detail the traditional assumptions of human exemplarity in educational thought.

CHAPTER 2

The Historical Tradition of Human Exemplarity

Its Contributions and Assumptions

In the historical tradition of Western educational thought, discourse surrounding human exemplarity can be classified into two major conceptual categories. These categories relate to how human examples are said to function educationally. First, there exists a long tradition of understanding examples as being models for imitation. Examples function in education by revealing a pattern that can be reproduced in subsequent action. Second, there exists a tradition that emphasizes the nonimitative role of human examples in human development. This second way of understanding examples has often been advanced in opposition to the first and, although this position has fewer representatives, it has been argued with equal fervor and conviction. An examination of both strands of the tradition reveals a variety of productive ways of thinking about human exemplars in human learning. Within these proposals, however, there is a certain set of assumptions that should be interrogated.

IMITATIVE MODELS OF HUMAN EXEMPLARITY: THE STANDARD MODEL

Homer, the towering figure who stands behind all ancient educational discourse in the West, must begin any discussion of the history of human exemplarity. The educational importance of human lives within the Homeric epics centers on their uses as examples to be imitated. Homer is significant in educational exemplarity because he supplies some of the most influential models in the historical tradition. Indeed, the heroes of Homer became the focus of imitation throughout the Classical world. This remained true long after Greek and Roman society had moved beyond any overt endorsement of Homeric ethics. Indeed, even when the actions of the Homeric heroes had been deeply allegorized and reconceptualized to avoid the questionable moral implications of their conduct, their role as models for imitation was retained in an abstract form. In the words of historian H. I. Marrou, these heroes forever "haunted the Greek soul" (1956, p. 34).

The Homeric epics supplied not only the content of a pedagogy centered on human examples, but also the form of the pedagogy. At several points in the Homeric poems, we are presented with a young man who is initiated into the heroic life and its accompanying ethos. The initiation usually involves an experienced teacher or mentor who places the idea of a hero in front of the fledgling warrior and urges imitation. In the *Iliad*, the aged tutor Phoenix places the hero Meleager before Achilles in hopes of turning the enraged youth away from his anger against Agamemnon and back to the heroic obligations owed to his Achaean companions-in-arms (see *Iliad* 9: 646–729). In the *Odyssey*, an explicit pedagogy based on examples is even more pronounced. The goddess Athena places the hero Orestes before Odysseus' son, Telemachos, and urges Telemachos to avenge his lost and disrespected father. Athena tells Telemachos:

> Or have you not heard what glory was won by the great Orestes
> among all mankind, when he killed the murderer of his father,
> the treacherous Aigisthos, who had slain his famous father:
> So you too dear friend, since I can see you are big and splendid,
> be bold also, so that in generations to come they will praise you.
> (*Odyssey* 1: 298-303)†

With this injunction, Athena reveals a pattern for teaching and learning from human lives. The educational scheme proceeds as an excellent act is presented to the learner (defeating the "treacherous Aigisthos"), a description of the rewards that flow from the vision of excellence is described (in this case, the glory that Orestes won in avenging his father), and a challenge, in the form of a conclusion, is given to replicate the action ("so be bold also").

This process of (a) representing a person's actions, (b) relating the benefits that have come from the action, and then (c) using these benefits to motivate the student to be like the model, has been one of the most popular ways of thinking about role models in education. It can be found, for example, in everything from Plutarch's ancient moral biographies to 20th-century theories of "vicarious reinforcement" (where the rewards or punishment bestowed on a model is motivational to an observer). It is so fashionable that I will call it the *standard model* of thinking about human exemplars and imitation.

Because of the influential Homeric legacy, the role of the poet was defined in terms of education and education was understood in terms of the imitation of heroes. The poet becomes a teacher who educates by glorifying the heroes of old. Plato says in the *Phaedrus* that the poet "clothes all the great deeds accomplished by the men of old with glory, and thus educates those who come after" (245s). Plato himself adopts Homer's pedagogy by offering his own sort of hero. Plato's poetic dialogues generally exalt a new type of exemplar, the philosopher Socrates, the true lover of wisdom, rather than the passionate Achilles or the wily Odysseus. The main point of the Platonic dialogues, it could even be argued, is not to establish a philosophical doctrine but to present a new way of living. One should imitate Socrates, the Platonic dialogues seem to imply, by living a rigorous philosophical life. In the character of Socrates, Plato seems to enact poetically what his student Aristotle would later explicitly theorize: Human exemplars give us unique access to comprehending a life of virtue. The philosophers, in this sense, retained a very Homeric way of thinking about education.

Educating through examples was not only a central task of the Classical poets and philosophers, but also the historians. The Roman historian Livy (59 BC–17 AD) would frame his *History of Rome* by saying that the purpose of history is to give truthful accounts of "examples of every possible type." "From these," he writes in his preface, "you may select for yourself and your country what to imitate, and also what, as being mischievous in its inception and disastrous in its issues, you are to avoid." History is the study of possible human models. One examines the past, reflects on which actions have produced the best positive results (both with respect to oneself and to one's community), and then selects the model for imitation based on those results. The standard model of education has spread, it seems, from the poet, to the philosopher, to the historian.

Isocrates (436–338 BC), one of the most important teachers of rhetoric in the Classical world, adopts the use of human examples as

very limited approach
↳
anecdotal

one of his principal pedagogical devices and often uses the standard model of imitation in his writings. In a move to unify the scattered Greek polities against outside conquest, Isocrates writes a letter addressed to King Phillip of Macedonia, urging him to pattern his life after that of his father, who achieved political power through the noble pathway of friendship rather than through engendering factions and bloodshed. After describing the positive consequences the flowed from this strategy ("a long and happy life"), he concludes by saying, "Now, while all who are blessed with understanding ought to set before themselves the greatest of men as their model, and strive to become like him, it behooves you above all to do so" ("To Phillip," 106–13). In this passage, Isocrates offers a perfect replication of the standard model of teaching through human examples, and he also indicates that, for him, the imitative life is not for those who lack the courage or intelligence to choose their own way. It is not a derivative, second-hand type of education. Instead, he says that those who have "understanding" seek to imitate examples. Isocrates is elevating the status of imitative learning to a point that would later provoke a good deal of criticism. According to Isocrates, the imitation of exemplars is not opposed to living with intelligence; instead, imitating noble exemplars *is* intelligent living.

The Classical writers not only believed that imitation was compatible with sound judgment, but also that imitation was compatible with human freedom. In the famous satirical writings of Lucian of Samosota (120–180 AD), we have a description of his ideal philosopher, a man named Demonax. Even as a boy Demonax was known for despising "all that men count good" and for unreservedly cultivating "liberty and free speech" (Lucian, 1913 version, p. 149). Philosophy was understood, for Lucian and other Hellenistic thinkers, principally in terms of freedom of thought and action. Lucian emphasizes how all of Athens admired Demonax and viewed him as a superior being. He urges young philosophers to copy Demonax and to pattern their lives after his. For modern readers there seems to be some irony, of course, in expecting young people to learn "liberty and free speech" by copying somebody else. Lucian describes Demonax's liberty as an essential feature of his philosophic life and holds out this freedom as itself something that can and should be imitated. As with Isocrates, later critics would take exception to this and argue that if someone were truly free, he or she could not be simply copying another person. Imitation, they would say, is a form of enslavement. But Lucian, for one, does not seem to find liberty and imitation as conceptually incompatible.

Writers in the Middle Ages drew on the Classical emphasis on imitation, infusing it with relevant Biblical teachings.[2] Particularly in the 11th and 12th centuries, the driving force in medieval education was the charismatic presence of the teacher that provoked an imitative response in the students. Stephen Jaeger (1994) has argued that, in early medieval pedagogical schemes, the personal attractiveness of the teacher was highly emphasized: "The physical presence of the educated man possessed a high pedagogic value; his composure and bearing, his conduct of life, themselves constituted a form of discourse, intelligible and learnable" (p. 80). Educated people did not write books in this era, but demonstrated their learning by living in a certain way. Exterior bodily features manifest an interior order, and virtue was thought to be exhibited by how one walked, talked, and held oneself: "Life itself," in other words, "could become a work of philosophy" (p. 85).[3] Imitation of these exterior bodily actions was seen as a way to acquire inner virtue (and, equally important, also a way to gain higher political and ecclesiastical positions).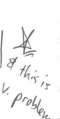

The importance of imitation in the educational thought of the Middle Ages is shown as authors emphasize the importance of selecting good models. The author of *Moralium dogma philosophorum* argues that we must "choose a good man and hold his image ever before our mind's eye" (quoted in Jaeger, pp. 79), as does the didactic poet Thomasin von Zirclaere (ca. 1215 AD), who asserts that a student should "choose in his mind an excellent man and arrange his behavior according to that pattern" (Jaeger, p. 79-80). In these passages, we see many elements of the standard model: an examination of a model's quality of life, a selection of a model based on that judgment, and a suggestion to imitate whomever is selected.

Although the emphasis on the embodied authority of the teacher waned in the later Middle Ages with the emergence of the scholastic ideals of rational inquiry and systematic texts, the educational importance of imitation lived on—though, as we shall see, it was looked upon with a much more critical eye. John Locke (1632–1704) would use the standard model in the very different intellectual climate of the Enlightenment. In his book, *Some Thoughts Concerning Education* (1692/2001), Locke argues that the easiest way to instruct children in manners is to "set before their eyes the examples of things you would have them do, or avoid; which when pointed out to them, in the practice of persons within their knowledge, with some reflections on their beauty and unbecomingness, are of more force to draw or deter their imitation, than any discourse which can be made to them" (§82). Like many others, Locke suggests that educators put examples of excellent human action before the youth, point out the beauty of the action, and then expect the subsequent imitation. The best type of exemplars, Locke assumes, are those persons "within the knowledge" of the children, suggesting that the exemplars should not be mythical heroes or great kings of the past, but should be drawn from the child's own life circumstances.

Notice, however, that Locke offers a different twist on the standard model. He starts from the assumption that children imitate any and all human behavior that is placed before them. Indeed, the educator should "put nothing before [the child] which you would not have him imitate" (§71). Accordingly, in his educational writings Locke does not say that the teacher must *exhort* imitation. The exhortation appears unnecessary. Instead of exhorting imitation and pointing to the model, the educator should carefully select what the learner sees. Since imitation seems to be an automatic human response, the exhortation stage of the standard model that comes after exposure to the exemplar is replaced by a selection phase in which the educator chooses what the child sees beforehand. The centrality of imitation, though, remains constant.

ENLIGHTENMENT CRITICISM AND NONIMITATIVE EXEMPLARS

According to the standard model and its variations, human examples give *information* about how to live successfully. This information may relate to the possibility and value of a certain way of life, or it may be about how to do specific actions. The information offered by examples may also be abstracted beyond the specific actions of the model and taken up in different contexts and practices. All of these informational aspects of human exemplars in the standard model are placed within a wider context of imitation. The information is about how to live; the model's life is taken as an example of a possible life that the students can have through imitation. The information is valuable because the observer can, in at least some sense, use the information to do the *same* thing the model did and thus reproduce the same achievements.

It is possible, however, to separate the educational value of exemplars from this imitative context. There has been a competing tradition of educational discourse that finds the educational importance of human exemplars to be in something other than in imitation. During the Enlightenment period, in particular, educational theorists became suspicious of the idea that examples were to be linked with imitation. It was still considered essential to observe and talk about examples of human lives, but they were not seen as models to be imitated. The human example, for many Enlightenment figures, does not provide information about a possible life to be adopted. The importance of the example lies elsewhere.

The decline of the imitative side of human exemplarity is related to the conceptions of human reason that developed in the modern era. The Enlightenment project is perhaps best exemplified in René Descartes's (1596–1650) goal of building knowledge on unshakeable foundations. Discovering that he had been taught certain errors during his youth, Descartes opted for a method of systematic doubt and decided to trust only what he himself could understand and justify. Descartes's desire was to separate his knowledge from the fallibility of social opinion and to ground his belief on a more objective foundation. He found surety within himself as a thinking being, that is, he found surety in his transcendental ego the existence of which could not be doubted. From this perch of certainty, the ego could stand back from the social world and pass judgment on it. This epistemic individualism that Descartes exemplified broke the tie to normative traditions that had been so essential to the ancient world.

This break with past traditions also reshaped the role of human examples in education, although the implications of Enlightenment epistemic individualism only gradually entered into educational theory. As I pointed out, educational theorists like John Locke still endorsed imitation. But Locke also wrestled with doubts about its value. Imitative action, he came to conclude, meant nothing if it was not tied to the true inclinations of the individual self. He writes in *Some Thoughts Concerning Education* that some students "endeavour to make shew of dispositions of mind, which they have not, but to express those they have by a carriage not suited to them" (§66). He continues, "Imitation of others, without discerning what is graceful in them, or what is peculiar to their characters, often makes a great part of this." Pretending to have qualities we do not through imitation is greatly offensive, he says, because "we naturally hate whatever is counterfeit." For Locke, imitative behavior can superficially mask a defect or mistake within the true self; the self becomes a forgery. For this reason, Locke says that imitation should only exist when paired with a certain discernment; namely, the ability to see "what is graceful" or "what is peculiar" in the exemplars. People should be able to look inside the example and see the character from which the actions spring. The true inner character of the imitator then needs to match that of the model.

The fear that imitation is the betrayal of a true self, raised in a mild way by Locke, is voiced again in a more forceful way by Jean-Jacques Rousseau (1712–1778). For Locke, imitation may be bad if it is "counterfeit," that is, if the qualities of the imitator's inner self do not match the inner qualities of the model. In his book, *Emile*, Rousseau takes an even stronger position that, for children, almost all imitation is a betrayal of proper human existence. Modern society corrupts, and imitation is a movement toward this society and away from the natural man that constitutes proper human nature. Children should live according to nature, not according to the actions of other people. "In choosing objects for imitation," he writes, "I would always take nature as my model" (Rousseau, 1762/1979, p. 345). Rousseau believes that the "foundation of imitation among us comes from the desire always to be transported out of ourselves." He continues, "If I succeed in my enterprise, Emile surely will not have this desire. We must, therefore, give up the apparent good which imitation can produce" (p. 104).

Imitation of examples, according to many Enlightenment thinkers, makes people alien in their own skin. For Locke the danger of imitation is the possibility of being counterfeit; for Rousseau the danger lays in being forgetful:

> I see from the way young people are made to read history that they are transformed, so to speak, into all the persons they see; one endeavors to make them become now Cicero, now Trajan, now Alexander, and to make them discouraged when they return to themselves, to make each of them regret being only himself. This method has certain advantages which I do not discount; but, as for my Emile, if in these parallels he must once prefer to be someone other then himself—were this Socrates, were it Cato— everything has failed. He who begins to become alien to himself does not take long to forget himself entirely. (1762/1979, p. 243)

Teaching with examples makes students dissatisfied with themselves and this is directly contrary to Rousseau's educational goals. Human exemplars are used by Rousseau in educating Emile, of course, but all the heroes are presented and then simultaneously undermined—the rural children, Robinson Crusoe, and the Spartans all meet the same fate. Rousseau does urge Emile's tutor to be an example, but that is only because the tutor is himself imitating the young, natural Emile. Emile, in imitating the tutor, is really only imitating himself. "In the morning let Emile run barefoot in all seasons, in his room, on the stairs, in the garden," he says. "Far from reproaching him, I shall imitate him" (1762/1979, p. 139). In fact, the tutor is chosen precisely because he is a future Emile. Rousseau thus believes that his sort of imitation, and only this sort, avoids the danger of forgetfulness.

Rousseau's suspicion of imitation does not mean that he deemphasizes human exemplarity. Quite the contrary: As Irene Harvey (2002) points out, a discourse of exemplarity pervades every corner of the text. Human examples play an important role in constituting Emile's sense of self. Harvey points to Rousseau's description of Emile's encounter with an angry man. When Emile asks about the encounter, the tutor is to say that anger is an example of "sickness" and sickness exemplifies the natural order of things. Through the example, he is taught to interpret himself and his relationship to the world. He is not told, however, to imitate the human example by becoming angry. Examples come to constitute his way of seeing rather than his way of acting. Examples continue to permeate Emile's existence, even though he does not follow the examples.

Immanuel Kant (1724–1804) finds a central place for imitation in his educational thought, but imitation is ultimately a betrayal of the fullest expression of rational human nature. It is true that, for Kant, "learning is nothing but imitation" (1790/1987, p. 176). Examples are important for Kant for several reasons. They strengthen judgment (*Geisteskraft*), provide useful metaphors, supply hope and inspiration, or serve as reminders of ideals (Louden, 1992). In moral education, Kant says that imitation is essential for an "undeveloped human being" because it is "the first determination of his will to accept maxims that he afterwards makes for himself." But moral maxims must, in fully rational human beings, be autonomous (i.e., self-legislated): "For, a maxim of virtue consists precisely in the subjective autonomy of each human being's practical reason and so implies that the law itself, not the conduct of other human beings, serves as our incentive" (1797/1983, p. 148). Kant thus criticizes a model of imitation in which the fact that others are doing an action is the reason for the action. Exemplars, in cases such as these, are heteronomous forces standing opposed to the autonomous will. For Kant, doing an action merely because someone else does it is a violation of free human reason. You should not learn morality "from experience" or be "taught it by other men"; rather, "your own reason teaches you what you have to do and directly commands it" (1797/1964, pp. 154–55).[4] To imitate is to contradict the faculty of reason that makes us who we are.

But there is another reason why Kant is suspicious of learning from exemplars. In direct opposition to someone like Aristotle, Kant says that examples must be judged by general norms, which are not discovered through observation and empirical inquiry. To emphasize examples is to put the proverbial cart before the horse. Kant believes that "every example presented to me must first itself be judged by moral principles in order to decide if it is fit to serve as . . . a model: it can in no way supply the prime source for the concept of morality" (quoted in Louden, 1998). Principles always come before examples, for Kant, because principles tell us what a "good" example is.

In the *Critique of Judgment*, human examples are further discussed in their relationship to genius. Kant believes that "genius is entirely opposed to the spirit of imitation" (1790/1987, p. 176). Kant defines a work of genius as that which cannot be arrived at by following a rule. Even if a scientist makes a grand discovery, in Kant's view, it is probably not a work of genius, especially if the scientist was following the preexisting rules of a "scientific method." For Kant, it is the revolutionary artist who is the real genius—only the artist produces creative works that are not simply the product of the application of method. Kant thinks that imitation is a sort of method consisting of "doing what X does, because X does it" and therefore stands in stark contrast to genius.[5]

It is fairly easy, I believe, for modern readers to understand why Kant degrades imitative action. If I learn to play the piano by slavishly imitating a master pianist, my playing will necessarily be derivative. Imitation, freedom, and creative action often do seem irreconcilable. If I am doing what somebody else does, I cannot be acting freely or creatively. Imitating exemplars, then, seems to prevent the emergence of humanity's uppermost capabilities and highest plateaus of rational development. Examples are necessary at first, Kant admits, but human beings should eventually grow out of the need to imitate. Kant would disagree sharply with the Classical writers who believed imitation to be compatible with creative judgment and with human freedom.

Ralph Waldo Emerson (1803–1882), in his early years, was perhaps the severest critic of imitating examples. His famous essay "Self Reliance" could be taken as an extended attack on imitation in all of its varieties. "There is a time in every man's education," he writes, "when he arrives at the conviction that envy is ignorance; that imitation is suicide; that he must take himself for better, for worse, as his portion; that though the wide universe is full of good, no kernel of nourishing corn can come to him but through his toil bestowed on that plot of ground which is given to him to till" (1841/1982, p. 176). He echoes Rousseau's sentiments that imitation is an alienation from the true self, corrupting the intellect: "We imitate; and what is imitation but the traveling of the mind? Our houses are built with foreign taste; our shelves are garnished with foreign ornaments; our opinions, our tastes, our faculties, lean, and follow the Past and the Distant"

(p. 198). Imitating exemplars is not only a counterfeit action and a forgetfulness, but also a suicide. It kills the here and now.

Yet even Emerson finds a place for human exemplars in his later book *Representative Men*. Observing great exemplars helps us to rejoice in the possibilities of human life: "In one of those celestial days when heaven and earth meet and adorn each other, it seems a poverty that we can only spend it once: We wish for a thousand heads, a thousand bodies, that we might celebrate its immense beauty in many ways and places. Is this fancy? Well, in good faith, we are multiplied by our proxies" (p. 8). Indeed: "We are tendencies, or rather, symptoms, and none of us complete. We touch and go, and sip the foam of many lives. Rotation is the law of nature" (p. 11). As we observe lives around us— as we sip the foam of others' examples—we gain a greater sense of the possible scope of human existence. In this way, Emerson believes that the great exemplars play a celebratory role in human life. They change us for the better, but not because we imitate their actions. Great individuals help us to better understand the varieties of human action and thus we come to better appreciate human existence.

In addition to this vicarious celebration of possibility, Emerson argues that human exemplars allow us to see the world through new eyes. The end of human exemplarity is not replicating an observed action; rather, the benefit of exemplarity is that it opens up a new way of seeing. "Activity is contagious," Emerson writes. "Looking where others look, and conversing with the same things, we catch the charm which lured them." He continues: "Great men are thus a collyrium to clear our eyes from egotism and enable us to see other people and their works" (p. 15). As we watch people go about their lives, our attention shifts from the people to the objects that concerned the people. As we pay greater attention to these new objects of concern, we may begin to see what others see. Examples refine our perceptive abilities.

Emerson's thinking about the positive role of exemplarity echoes other Enlightenment figures. As Rousseau also seemed to indicate at various points, exemplars play a role in formulating questions in addition to granting answers. Of his representative men, Emerson writes, "I cannot tell what I would know; but I have observed there are persons who, in their character and actions, answer questions which I have not the skill to put" (p. 5). The examples of human lives offer answers, to be sure, but perhaps even more interesting are the questions that they reveal. They may open up new lines of inquiry that otherwise may not have been possible. As we see someone doing something extraordinary, for example, we are presented with new questions: What does it say about human beings that we are capable of this sort of achievement, this sort of folly, or this sort of evil?

Finally, with Kant, Emerson suggests that one purpose of remembering great individuals is not gaining information from the lives of others, but rather, gaining inspiration: "I cannot even hear of personal vigor of any kind, great power of performance," Emerson writes, "without fresh resolution" (p. 9). The point of exemplars is to reveal a level of achievement that all human beings can attain. He writes, "Men are also representative; first, of things, and secondly, of ideas" (1850/1996, p. 6). Exemplars represent certain truths about the world; they "incarnate" ideas, including the normative ideas that are to guide human life. They embody, however, particular types of normative ideas. For Emerson, Plato becomes "a great average man" in whom "men see . . . their own dreams and glimpses made available and made to pass for what they are." Men do not (or should not) desire to be Plato; instead, Plato transforms and rekindles their *own* dreams. Likewise, the point of reading Shakespeare is not to imitate his style, but to understand the "Shakespeare in us." People should not copy Shakespeare, but realize that we, too, can participate in his sort of creative achievements. The reason for great men to exist, and for their memory to be propagated, Emerson argues, is so "that there may be greater men" (p. 20). Great men inspire us to do our own great things, they do not ask us to imitate them.

As the Enlightenment wanes, we see Friedrich Nietzsche (1844–1900) echoing many themes of Emerson. Nietzsche condemns what he calls the "laziness" of people when they simply follow current opinions and conventions. Doing something because another person does it is to become part of a grotesque human "herd." To follow the herd is to value the life of pleasure and ease above the life of striving and achievement. At the same time, though, Nietzsche's writings reveal a vigorous search for a new human exemplar, one uncorrupted by otherworldly illusion and ready to fully face the Godless reality that is the human condition. Nietzsche is constantly cycling through exemplary possibilities: Wagner, Schopenhauer, and then finally his fictional Zarathustra.

Even from the beginning Nietzsche's question was simple: "Where among our contemporaries can all of us—scholars and nonscholars—find our moral exemplars and people of distinction, visible embodiments of all creative morality in this age?" (1874/1995, p 178). These exemplars are to be imitated in a sense. It is true we are to "take our examples" from them (p. 181). But, as with Emerson, this is a special type of imitation; it is an imitation that involves becoming not like the model, but becoming instead "those we are." Or rather, we become

like our models in the sense that we become who we are just like they
have become who they are. Examples provoke a productive process;
they instill an urge to shape oneself by engaging creatively with the
resources of the historical age. The exemplar's call to become "who
you are" presents an ideal of human life and stimulates an inquiry
aimed at self-knowledge and self-creation. It is imitation of the exemplar on a very abstract level.

Nietzsche's more optimistic approach to human exemplarity (or
at least more optimistic than, say, Rousseau or Kant) can partly be
explained by Nietzsche's doubt about the Enlightenment transcendental ego, an idea he explicitly attacks in *Beyond Good and Evil* (§16).
There is no self that can stand apart from its language and social
existence to evaluate exemplars. The examples we are exposed to shape
our categories of understanding and evaluation from the beginning.
Thus, for someone like Nietzsche, it is impossible to ignore the influences and the exemplars that come with social existence. The point of
philosophy, and of life more generally, is to learn to engage with these
social influences in creative ways. Nietzsche's point about the social
contextualization that must be present in any view of human development will prove critical to the proper understanding of human exemplars that I will advance in subsequent chapters. His point about
working creatively within a framework of exemplarity will also relate
to the final analysis of the value of imitative learning.

The Enlightenment and post-Enlightenment tradition, then, is
wary of the educational value of imitative action (or at least imitative
action that is not abstracted from particular actions). It is a betrayal of
the sacred human individual, even a suicide. At the same time, however, these writers show how human exemplars can still play a positive role in education. They argue that exemplars might (a) offer
reminders and clarification of human ideals, (b) serve as provocations
to inquiry and inspirations to our own action, and (c) open up new
ways of seeing significance in the world. Although the assumptions of
the Enlightenment on the issue of imitation deserve scrutiny, this strand
of the historical tradition has added a great deal to our understanding
of how we might learn from other human lives.

I have presented the tradition's discussions of human exemplarity in education in largely historical terms: Premodern thinkers often
had a more positive view of imitation than did the moderns. It would
be a mistake, though, to think that discourse surrounding imitation
was absent during the Enlightenment—as we have seen, even Locke,
one of the paradigmatic figures of philosophical modernity, promoted
the imitation of exemplars. It would also be a mistake to think that

nonimitative educational understandings of exemplars were absent
outside of the Enlightenment. The Classical and Medieval writers realized that human exemplars can serve an inspirational role[6] and help
shape new ways of seeing,[7] even though they usually saw this role in
a larger context of imitation. Rather than being two different historical
categories, then, these approaches to human exemplarity should be
seen as always coexisting conceptual categories. The Enlightenment
stress on epistemic individualism merely produced an alternate emphasis rather than a qualitatively different view of human exemplarity
and human learning.

THE HISTORICAL TRADITION: AN INITIAL ASSESSMENT

Even this brief description of the Western historical tradition reveals a
wide array of educational proposals relating to human examples. The
greatest contribution of the historical tradition, I have suggested, is
seen in the variety and richness of these suggestions. The tradition has
been less successful, however, in examining the assumptions about
human psychology, motivation, reason, and the process of exemplification that seem to underlie the suggestions. Although there have
been many significant proposals made about what human examples
can and should do, there has been little critical reflection on the underlying assumptions of these proposed models. In fact, the assumptions
of these models of exemplarity have rarely been identified, let alone
examined or critiqued. This holds true for both the standard model of
imitative learning and the counterproposals made by critics of imitation such as those in the Enlightenment.

Consider first the standard model of learning from examples that
I have described. This model contains three main elements: the description of an example's action, the description of the results of the
action, and an exhortation to do what the example did. This way of
thinking makes certain assumptions about how learning from examples
proceeds. It assumes that two elements are at work in the functioning
of imitative learning: (a) a cognitive aspect, which selects and represents the important aspects of the model's actions or goals, and (b) an
affective element, which gives the learner a certain feeling of attraction
toward the cognitive representation—we could also call this the motivational element of exemplarity.

Under the standard model, the cognitive element of imitative
learning is supplied when attention is drawn to the exemplar's actions
and to the results that flow from the actions, thus allowing the ob-

server to construct a mental representation of the actions and their consequences. The model is framed as an example of something as the teacher draws attention to the example's actions. Once the attention has been properly focused, the motivational element enters as the observer considers the action's consequences. If the results are attractive, they inspire the observer to replicate the action. In short, the exhortational element of the standard model involves telling the learner to pay attention to the action and its results, while the consequences supply the motivation to imitate the action. The assumptions underlying this process of imitation merit close scrutiny.

The Assumption of Consequential Motivation

One obvious assumption of the standard model is this: Seeing the results of the model's action is the key motivator in initiating an imitative response. I will call this "the assumption of *consequential motivation*." At first, this assumption seems quite defensible. While fishing, I do often imitate the lures used by fishermen who seem to be having the most successful outcomes—seeing them actually catch fish (something I am not good at) motivates my imitation.[8] For these observed outcomes to function motivationally, however, it seems necessary that the outcome be desirable for the learner and also be deemed a real possibility in the context of the learner. Motivation would fail, under this model, if the outcome is something the learner does not want, or if it is something that does not appear possible for the learner. If I for some reason did not want to catch fish, or if I were fishing in an area that I believed contained a different type of fish than the model was catching, then the information about successful lures would not necessarily motivate me to replicate the use of the lure.

Even with these qualifications it seems that the assumption of consequential motivation has limited explanatory power. It does not account for many instances of imitation. Sometimes an action may be imitated even without any idea of the resulting consequences. This seems to be the case with acquiring accented English when living abroad or picking up another person's turn-of-phrase. Picking up a particular turn-of-phrase may not lead to *any* apparent consequences, and yet we may start imitating the language use anyway. We may even start to imitate those actions that we know to have negative consequences, thinking that things will be different in our case. So the assumptions of the standard model of imitative learning do not seem to hold for all cases of imitative learning. This is to suggest that motivation to imitate is not always born from a rational, means-to-ends analysis of how to get what we want, as the assumption of consequential motivation implies. But if imitative motivation does not always follow this process, how else might it arise? This question of how motivation enters into the imitation of human exemplars is a question that requires more serious engagement.

The Assumption of Intentional Selection

This standard model also seems to assume that human exemplarity can be actualized in the mind of the learner through an act of "pointing," physically or verbally, to the exemplar or by placing an example in front of the learner. The teacher can "clothe the great deeds in glory," as Plato says, and thereby make the deeds serve as examples. I will call this "the assumption of *intentional selection*." A teacher, according to this assumption, has *control* over which actions are taken to be exemplary and which are not. It also implies that we, when we function as self-educators, choose our own examples. Thus, the standard model presupposes the possibility of selection and makes certain assumptions about how things become exemplary in the minds of learners. Examples become examples, it has often been assumed in education writing, simply when we want to use them as examples. Alternatively, there is the more Lockean theory that everything that is placed before us becomes an example, and the intentions of the teacher are expressed in selecting what the learner sees. Both theories, in different ways, presuppose that teachers have control over what becomes an example.

But does the assumption of intentional selection hold up? As was pointed out in the first chapter, a person can simultaneously embody many different characteristics and be an example on many different levels of abstraction. When we say, "Be like the example," how does a learner know which aspect of the example we are pointing to? Or if we place an example before the eyes of a student, how are we to be sure that attention is focused on the intended characteristics? It seems there must be more to the idea of a student selecting an example than just being directed by the gestures or exhortations of a teacher. Thus, another major question to ask is how instances of a thing become *examples* of the thing. We also need to examine, it seems, this assumption of intentional selection.

The Assumption of Reason's Incompatibility with Imitation

The critics of imitation, such as those in the Enlightenment tradition, also seem to make questionable assumptions. The critics of imitative exemplarity assume a wide divide between imitative action, which they see as always nonrational and derivative, and action that is creative, autonomous, and independent. This brings up questions of how exemplars function in the process of human reason, and whether they function in a way that is troublingly nonrational or even irrational. In what ways can imitation play a role in human reason? Is imitation a poor substitute for individual practical wisdom? Does it violate human autonomy? The contested nature of the relationship between imitation and reason brings up larger questions about the value of imitation. I have already noted that many in the Classical tradition believed that the judicious imitation of examples was by itself an intelligent activity, so a negative assessment of imitation in this regard has not always been the obvious one. The Classical tradition also held that imitation was compatible with human freedom. An answer to the question of where exemplarity fits into human reason, I believe, lies in understanding how imitative action changes and sculpts human life and communities. To decide whether imitation can play a positive role in human reason, and to decide the value of imitation overall, we need to understand the meaning of imitation within communities.

These questionable assumptions all involve questions relating to the nature of the self. The imitative model of human exemplarity often assumes that the self makes judgments about who to select as an example based on rational means-to-ends analysis. But is this really the way the process works? In other words, is the self fundamentally a rational chooser? For their part, the critics of exemplarity (such as those of the Enlightenment) tend to assume a transcendent self standing apart from social influence that imitative action can corrupt. But is there such a self? Can the self stand back from what surrounds it and select which people are taken as examples and what these people are examples of? Recent trends in philosophy tend to emphasize that the only self that exists is a socially constituted self—one that is heavily involved in traditions and normative exemplars from the very beginning. To assume that the "self" has any independent existence apart from its participation in traditions, languages, and forms of life is problematic. Rethinking imitation will require rethinking the nature of the self and the existence of the self in society.

CHAPTER 3

How Do People Become Examples?

There is something about the ability to see things as examples that is intimately tied to education, and not just because teachers sometimes use examples in explicit instruction. Some have equated the capacity to be influenced by examples as precisely the capacity to learn. The ability to recognize things as examples of something else in increasing levels of complexity could, indeed, be an interesting definition of education. To see a particular something as an example of a more general phenomenon is to make a connection between oneself and other people, between past and present, between local and distant, or between theory and practice. This ability to see examples may be manifest in many ways: seeing rust as an example of oxidization, seeing a star as an example of a red giant, or seeing a cowardly act as an example of moral failure. The ability to simultaneously see one thing as exemplifying multiple categories (to see a rainbow as an example of light's refraction, of natural beauty, of divine promises in ancient traditions, and so forth) is perhaps a mark of what we call a liberal education. The functioning of exemplarity is central, in this sense, to discourse surrounding human development and education.

This chapter examines how we come to see other people as examples. Recall that the standard model assumes what I have called "intentional exemplarity." This is the assumption that human beings become examples as a teacher highlights their significant attributes. Intentional exemplarity implies that our beliefs about a person are what allow the person to function as our example. We believe a person is superior to us in certain way and we therefore intentionally select that person to be our example (those beliefs that allow us to humbly accept instruction from others have been called "tutelary beliefs"). Let us take this assumption of intentional motivation, together with its focus on tutelary belief as a starting point, and work backward to the basic elements of this assumption.

Perhaps the first question that arises when we consider the function of human exemplarity is this: When teachers highlight another person as an example, what exactly are they intending that person to be an example of? An initial response to this question can be seen in the writings of Rousseau. In her study of Rousseau's *Emile,* Irene Harvey outlines the ontological structure of exemplarity for Rousseau and suggests that the nature of human exemplarity consists in seeing the other as a possible example of a future self. When we see somebody act as an example, we link "the act of the other to its possibility for me as my act in some future situation" (2002, p. 123). We see the action not simply as somebody else doing the action, but as ourselves possibly doing the same action at some point in the future. The action, in other words, "becomes pregnant with my future possibility" (p. 123).

This seems to be a productive way of thinking about human exemplarity. Human examples function in education as representations of a self that is not yet realized. They act as mirrors that reflect not who we currently are, but who we could one day be. Through examples, we come to see our future selves in those around us. Of course, a future self is not the only thing that human examples are taken to represent. For instance, a human example can function educationally as being *not me* ("that action is not what I want to do") or it can have nothing to do with me at all, but with *us* ("that person is how *we all* should be"). Additionally, an educational human example can be an example of a *past me,* a representation of what I once was, but no longer am. This type of exemplary structure can be particularly instructive ("that person is an example of how I used to be, and I now see how ridiculous I looked"). But human examples exert much of their power when they appear as a possible future self—a telos adopted for a possible developmental process to come.

The idea that human exemplars are representations of future selves can only take us so far, though, in explaining how things become examples. After all, how is it that a person becomes an example of anything, even apart from being an example of future self? Before we can even begin to analyze the assumption of intentional exemplarity, there are more basic questions that need to be addressed: What does it mean to say that X is an example of Y? Is possession of a trait sufficient to make something an *example* of something with that trait? If not, how is it that things come to exemplify the traits that they possess? And how does this translate into examples of human beings?

THE NATURE OF EXAMPLES

Starting with the Greeks, there have been two prominent ways of understanding the exemplarity relationship. Plato understands what we call an "example" (in Greek *paradeigma*) to be "a pattern or model of a thing to be executed," such as an artistic model or a legal precedent (Liddell & Scott, 1964, p. 595). This is related to Plato's theory of Forms: Examples are the transcendental archetypes that shape and give meaning to the earthly particulars that derive from them. The relationship for Plato is one in which the example somehow sets the standard for the particulars. Aristotle adds to this view a more rhetorical understanding of examples. Examples for Aristotle are particulars that point to a general category or conclusion: "for the example," he writes in *Rhetoric*, "is induction" (I. II. 8). The example is taken to be a particular piece of a larger collection of parts or an instance of a general rule. Aristotle says, for instance, that an orator may use the examples of past kings who attacked Greece after first conquering Egypt to argue that the Greeks should not allow a foreign king to overcome Egypt (*Rhetoric*, II. XX. 3–5). In contrast to the Platonic usage, then, Aristotle argues that examples can function as persuasive samples—a sample of a cake can serve as a type of inductive evidence about the general quality of the cake from which the sample is taken.

Under this Aristotelian understanding of the exemplarity relationship, the example is *one* part of a greater whole (one part of the many that could be chosen) whereas in the Platonic understanding the example is the *One*—the general paradigm from which the particulars derive. The single example has a normative power in the Platonic understanding of exemplarity in a way that it does not in the Aristotelian. Thus, as Gelley points out, ideas of exemplarity have long mixed the "singular with the normative" (1995, p. 2). Growing out of this mixture is a multifaceted understanding of exemplarity in contemporary discourse.

The first contemporary understanding of an "example" relates more to the Aristotelian conception of an example as one particular slice of a larger whole. If we think of examples in this way, an example of a trait is anything that possesses that trait. Anyone who clearly possesses the trait of courage, for instance, could thus be an example

ge, just like any book could serve as an example of a book. Any particular member of a group can be an example of that group's larger membership under this way of thinking about examples. The second, more Platonic understanding of examples sees examples in a more normative way. Indeed, examples establish the norm for something, and this norm sets the standard by which other instances of that something are judged. Not every book is an example of a book and not every person who exhibits violence is an example of violence. The particular example casts judgment on and serves as the standard by which the other instances within a group are judged. The finely printed, leatherbound classic Victorian novel becomes the exemplar that makes the connoisseur frown upon the paperback romance in the bargain bin of the bookstore.

These two views of examples imply a different sort of relationship between parts and wholes, generals and particulars. The Platonic view posits that the relationship is normative while the more Aristotelian view sees the relationship as simply sharing a class or group membership. By using the term "induction," however, Aristotle seems to have a more specific view of the relationship between parts and wholes. Aristotle's notion that examples are inductive implies a certain sort of *communicative* relationship between parts and whole. For an example to be inductive—for a part to give us access to the whole—the particular must effectively refer to the whole. If swans are to be an example of a "white bird" then they must effectively communicate the linkage between being white and being a bird. Under a more refined Aristotelian view, then, examples are still parts of wholes, but they are also parts that are able to communicate their relevant attributes.

The more refined Aristotelian view seems to more fully describe how we most often think about examples. The Christian philosopher St. Augustine describes a case that illustrates this point. He asks how we might try to show someone what it meant to "walk." Usually, if we wanted to be an example of walking, we would simply get up and walk around in front of whoever made the inquiry. We would try to show by example. Augustine points out, though, that as we are walking around, we are really showing an almost infinite number of different actions. "How shall I," he wonders, "avoid having the asker think that walking consists in walking only so far as I walked?" (1948 version, p. 385). I may be modeling the activity of walking, after all, but I also may technically be walking ten steps, walking without a limp, walking in order to teach, and so forth. The same holds true, as was pointed out in chapter 1, if we watch Gavrilo Princip shoot the Archduke Franz Ferdinand. Any action is concurrently instantiating a large number of features. Surely all of these features are not exemplified, or at least not exemplified in the same way. It seems odd to say that I am an example of "walking ten steps" every time I walk ten steps: At most, I am a potential example of walking ten steps. We tend to think of examples, then, as being more than simply particular slices of a larger group or whole that possesses certain features. Something else is required.

Consider a cloth sample in a fabric store. The sample has many traits—color, pattern, weave, size, date of production, and so on. However, we usually do not think that all of these traits are exemplified in the sample. For a customer in the fabric shop, the sample is taken to exemplify color, pattern, and weave, but it is usually not taken to be an example of size or date of production. The sample may have come from cloth that was finished on Tuesday, but it would be odd if someone in the fabric store would take the sample as an example of something "finished on Tuesday." Under the fuller understanding of exemplarity, something is an example only to the extent that it communicates the features it possesses.

Some recent Anglo-American philosophers have developed this communicative idea at some length. Nelson Goodman's book, *Languages of Art*, argues that examples must exhibit *possession* plus *reference*. To be an example, in other words, a thing must possess or instantiate a predicate (it must be, say, red). And it must also communicate or refer that predicate (it must highlight the idea of redness). "To have without symbolizing is merely to possess," he writes, "while to symbolize without having is to refer in some other way than by exemplifying" (1997, p. 53). The exemplarity relationship consists in possessing the trait that is exemplified *and* in expressing the idea of that trait. A cloth sample in a fabric store may possess the trait of being "made on Tuesday," but it does not express the idea of that trait and is not, therefore, taken as an example of being "made on Tuesday."

Katherine Elgin (1991) helpfully illustrates this point. All paints, she says, possess the feature of viscosity, but not all instances of paint give us examples of viscosity. Only certain uses of paint, such as a Jackson Pollock painting, serve to exemplify viscosity, even though it is a feature that all other paintings possess. She writes:

> [T]hrough its clots and streaks, dribbles and spatters, the Pollock makes a point of viscosity. Most other paintings do not. They use or tolerate viscosity, but make no comment on it. To highlight, underscore, display, or convey involves reference as well as instantiation. (1991, p. 198)

Elgin argues that examples are usually thought to give us "epistemic access" to what they exemplify. The cloth sample that was made on Tuesday does not give us access to the idea of being "made on Tuesday," even though it belongs to that class of objects. Thus, it is not an example of this trait.

The Goodman tradition seems to correctly describe the way examples communicate general features. A human example, according to this tradition, would be a person that instantiated and referred a particular predicate. Thus, to exemplify generosity, a person must be generous and must be generous in a way that underscores, displays, or conveys the idea of generosity to an observer. The referential aspect of the example allows an observer epistemic access to the quality and sets the stage for the inclusion of this quality into the idea of a normative future self. A person who is "generous," but does not somehow convey generosity, is not an example. Since the person is not an example of generosity, she cannot serve as an example of a generous future self for those who observe her actions. The same holds true for a person who is violent: Not everyone who is violent is an example of violence. This fact will have implications for how we think about media violence.

Notice that the part-whole relationship is still assumed in the Goodman tradition. In order for something to exemplify it must instantiate an existing predicate or label. When a color patch is offered as an example of something that is red, it is taken as a particular that communicates back toward the general label. When Gandhi is offered as a particular example of pacifism, his example refers back to the general predicate "pacifism." The example can communicate because of its connection to generally used terms, predicates, or categories.

Goodman goes on to make the controversial point that only predicates or labels are exemplified. Examples must relate to some sort of meaningful conceptual category. But this does not necessarily mean that only things for which we have words are exemplified. Indeed, Goodman acknowledges that the label may be nonlinguistic: "Symbols from other systems—gestural, pictorial, diagrammatic, etc.—may be exemplified and otherwise function much as predicates of a language" (p. 57). Still, exemplification "seems to derive from the organization of language even where nonverbal symbols are involved" (p. 57), and it must still be based on predicates and labels that are like language.[1]

One implication of this view is that, as our conceptualization of existing predicates changes, so also does the range of exemplification. Elgin argues, for example, that Cézanne only came to be an example of a "harbinger of Cubism" after the category of "Cubism" was created years after his death. New categories of predication change what something can rightfully be said to exemplify. Thus, as social meanings change, exemplarity fluctuates with them. Goodman offers a first indication that social context is central to understanding how exemplarity relationships function and that exemplarity escapes human intentions. Pointing to the same example will have different meanings in different times and places. The assumption of "intentional exemplarity" already appears to be in trouble. What something can possibility exemplify is bound, in some sense, by social context.

HOW DOES SOMETHING BECOME AN EXAMPLE?

I have argued that mere possession of a trait leads to exemplification of that trait only under a very limited understanding of exemplarity. Human beings are examples of their entire range of features only in the limited sense of examples being parts of larger wholes. That is to say, if by an "example" we mean just any particular part of a larger whole, then any particular possession of a trait is also an example of that trait. So the generous person is exemplifying generosity merely by instantiating that trait; the generous person is one part of a larger group of generous people. But this is not always how we think of exemplarity. Not every trait that something instantiates is also exemplified in the fuller understandings of exemplarity that I have stressed. Not every feature is exemplified because not every feature exists in a *communicative* relationship between the part and the whole.

How does as example become "telling" and thereby become an example in the second sense? Why is the fabric sample taken to exemplify color and texture, but not shape or date of production? Albert Bandura (1986) argues, correctly, that traits are modeled, or exemplified, when we pay a particular sort of attention to them. Something becomes an example, in other words, when we notice it in a certain way. It might be helpful, therefore, to frame the question of "telling" in terms of human attention. Examples catch our attention in a way that causes us to notice something about the thing's relationship to a broader group or general category. And it catches our attention in a way that offers some insight about the group or category. The fabric sample does not draw our attention to the trait of being "made on a Tuesday."

Bandura offers a few suggestions about how our attention can be captured by other people and, hence, how people can become examples of certain traits. Human actions, for instance, are more likely to grab our attention when (a) they are physically accentuated to high-light the important features and (b) when they are accompanied by a narration that reveals what is important (1986, p. 54). Under this un-derstanding of exemplarity, human beings become telling examples because their features make them conspicuous somehow or because somebody directs observers to pay attention to these features. Some-one exemplifies the trait of generosity by making the trait conspicuous through accentuating virtuous actions or by someone pointing out that the person is generous.

One idea that could be drawn from this, perhaps, is that some-thing becomes an example when it exaggerates a trait beyond average levels, since accentuation may sometimes be achieved through exag-geration. An example of a generous person would be someone who is even more generous than the average person. The more different some-one is from the norm, the more of an example the person becomes in her particular way of being different. Through exaggeration of a trait, our attention is drawn toward that trait (it becomes conspicuous) and this attention is what makes the thing become an example.

This sounds plausible but this surely cannot be the only way exemplarity is created. As Elgin argues, a bucket of paint spilled on the carpet would certainly be a conspicuous or exaggerated instance of paint's viscosity, but it is not a telling example of that feature. It would certainly draw our attention, to be sure, and the attribute of viscosity would be a part of what we were paying attention to. But our attention would not be focused on the idea of viscosity in such a way that information about that trait is revealed. It would be more focused on, say, saving the nearby carpet from getting ruined. Spilled paint catches our attention more as an example of an enormous mess than as an example of viscosity.

In human beings, then, the exaggeration of a trait does not nec-essarily qualify as an example of a trait (although it may in some circumstances). The figure of Santa Claus has the trait of generosity, no doubt, but Santa Claus is rarely ever held out as a moral exemplar to be imitated. One rarely hears children being told to be "be like Santa Claus." The exaggerated quality of the fictional character, manifest in giving gifts to all good children worldwide, does little to catch the moral attention. It is not so much that fictional and mythological char-acters cannot exemplify moral traits. Clearly they can. But this particu-lar fictional character for some reason does not seem to exemplify the trait even though it is extremely exaggerated instance of the trait.

Elgin offers her own ideas about how examples become commu-nicative of a certain trait. She points out, in contrast to the idea of exemplarity through exaggeration, that examples communicate by making known the "obscure or elusive features" rather than the glaring ones—an opera may have a conspicuously absurd plot yet may exemplify subtle emotions. So what is it that makes something communicate a trait so as to exemplify it? She writes, "[A telling example] presents those features in a context contrived to render them salient. This may involve unraveling common concomitants, filtering out impurities, clearing away unwanted clutter, presenting in unusual settings." She continues, "Stage setting can also involve introduction of additional factors. Thus a biologist stains a slide to bring out a contrast, and a composer elaborates a theme to disclose hidden harmonies" (1991, p. 199). When examples are telling, she reminds us, they provide "epistemic access" to the features exemplified. Thus, a flashlight can demonstrate the constancy of the speed of light, but it takes the Michelson-Morley experiment to exemplify this feature and to give us epistemic access to the principle. For Elgin, then, someone would become an example of generosity when she is placed in a context that renders that particular feature salient. A thing by itself is never an example, even if its features are highly exaggerated. An example requires a stage.

Although Elgin offers some ideas about how traits can come to be exemplified, she does not develop her ideas with much depth. She also does not discuss how things can be staged naturally and unintentionally merely by their situatedness within certain contexts. If we look closely at how things come to be examples, though, there appear to be two processes by which an instance of something becomes an example of something: convention and differentiation. Douglass Arrell has provided an explanation of how we know which qualities of the cloth sample in the fabric store are being exemplified. He writes, "When we perceive the piece of cloth as a sample . . . we have an unspoken agreement with the upholsterer to apply to it certain categories . . . but not others; that is to say, we submit to categorical constraint" (1990, p. 236). Social conventions and agreements, to be sure, may provide stages and frameworks—forms of life—that alert us to which aspects of a thing are being exemplified in a given situation and which are not. These stages are operative whether we want them to be or not.

Sometimes there is not any identifiable convention that informs what a particular thing is taken to exemplify. After all, which social conventions and agreements allow Pollack's *Number One* to exemplify viscosity? There may have been some, but they seem hard to pinpoint. The more interesting way to think about examples like these, I believe, is through "differentiation." According to this way of thinking about

no → relevance

exemplarity, something becomes an example because of the structures of similarity and difference within a given context. Many of the ways in which exemplification may happen—through exaggeration, filtering, placement in unusual settings, and so forth—promote exemplification because they highlight differences within a given situation. If this is true, then it is not the example itself that exemplifies; rather, the exemplification depends on the context of similarities and difference in which the example is placed.

The case of *Number One* as an example of viscosity suggests how this differentiation takes place. If all paintings were of the style of Pollock's *Number One*, this particular painting would cease to be an example of viscosity, even if the painting itself were to remain exactly the same. The painting exemplifies viscosity precisely because of its differences from other paintings within its group. The painting exemplifies this trait only because of its placement within the community. Arrell (1990) shows how exemplification works through differentiation by using several visual examples, which I have modified as part of Figure 3.1.

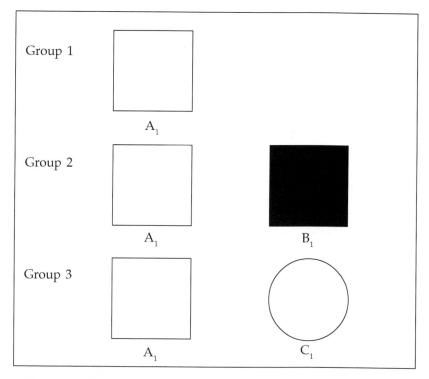

Figure 3.1. Exemplification and difference in group membership.

By itself, the object A_1 does not exemplify any particular trait. It is a white square of a certain size, it exists on a certain page, it was created on a certain day with the help of a word-processing application, it is part of a book about exemplarity and imitation, and so forth. It possesses all of these characteristics, but it does not yet exemplify any one of them. It does not make a point of any of these traits. Although convention does seem to mark its "squareness" as its most salient feature, it could yet be an example of a great number of things.

When this figure is placed in a context of similarity and difference, however, specific traits start to emerge as being exemplified. Consider the following pair of figures, A_1 and B_1. When A_1 stands alone in Group 1 it does not seem to exemplify anything. In the context of Group 2, however, A_1 now comes to exemplify "white" or "unshaded" as it is paired with B_1. The context of difference focuses our attention so that we see A_1 as an example of a larger category. Our attention is drawn to the color and thus the color becomes the subject of exemplification.

Arrell notes that when the object is placed in a different context, the exemplified trait shifts even though the object A_1 has not changed. When placed in a context that contains C_1, A_1 now can be said to exemplify its shape rather than its color. In a context of Group 3, in other words, A_1 now seems to be an example of squareness rather than of color. The example has changed because of where it has been grouped, and the context focuses our attention on certain features and away from others. These examples indicate that exemplification depends on the context of difference, then, within a particular setting.

Notice that the process of exemplification via differentiation has implications for both figures in the group. If A_1 is taken as an example of squareness within the particular group, then C_1 must be taken as an example of not-squareness (or of circularity if it is taken on its own terms). If exemplification is based on difference, then saying that something exemplifies a trait within a certain group is also implying that the other members of the group do not possess that trait in the same way. If A_1 is an example, then C_1 must in some sense be an example of not-A_1. To the extent that exemplarity is created through differentiation, to call something an example is also to simultaneously classify the other members of the group. Differentiation operates on the basis of inclusion and exclusion.

Having said this, one might be tempted to then say that difference itself is the deciding factor in exemplification. The more different something is, it may seem, the more it becomes an example with respect to the way in which it is different. This is the idea of exemplification through exaggeration in another guise, however, and we have already seen that there are problems with it. But if we wanted to create an example of a big square, we might still be tempted to put two squares together and then make one square of vastly greater size than the other. This is how someone might successfully indicate a "big square" when playing a game like charades or *Pictionary* (a board game in which people try to represent ideas pictorially). Indeed, it may be an effective strategy in this context; increasing the size difference may increase the likelihood that one square will be taken as an example of being big. So it again seems as if exaggerated difference is the most important factor in the functioning of exemplification. In the end, though, focusing on contextual differences misses how important similarity is in the exemplification process. Consider three more groups of figures, which I have represented in Figure 3.2.

As it stands alone in Group 1, the figure A₂ again does not seem to exemplify anything in particular. It could be a house, an arrow pointing up, and so forth. When placed in a context of both similarity

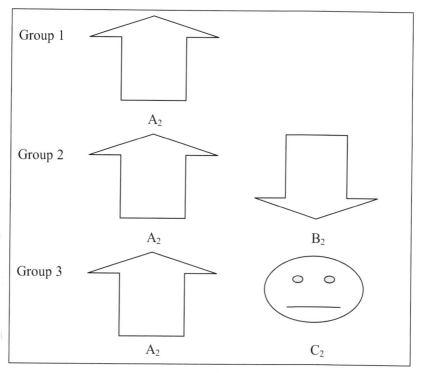

Figure 3.2. Exemplification and similarity in group membership.

and difference in Group 2, A_2 becomes an example of an "up arrow." The difference, again, draws our attention to certain features of the example. But when paired with C_2 in Group 3, it is much less clear what A_2 is an example of. The difference does not seem to stand out in this group in any way that allows for exemplarity; our attention fails to focus on any one feature. The figures are too different. It seems, therefore, that a context of similarity is just as important as difference in directing our attention toward examples. An exemplar has to be recognizably part of a community of things, but also recognizably different from other members of the community. *Number One* exemplifies viscosity only because of the community of paintings in which it stands.

With human exemplarity specifically, this analysis of differentiation and similarity continues to hold. After all, if other basketball players played "like Mike" (that is, like basketball star Michael Jordan), then Mike would cease to exemplify a particular style of play. The context of difference continues to matter a great deal. The context of similarity is also important with human examples. Again, not everybody who possesses an attribute to an extreme degree is an example of that attribute. Suppose we take generosity to mean giving gifts, especially gifts that are given at substantial personal cost. Someone who offers animal sacrifices to the Greek pantheon on behalf of others would probably not be considered an example of generosity in most current cultural contexts, even if the animal sacrifices were always done at great personal cost and with the purest altruistic intentions. If our munificent animal sacrificer existed in contemporary American society, for instance, he would probably not be considered an example of generosity. His gift would be so different that it would not be recognized as a gift within the social context. Since generosity is dependent on social practices like gift giving—what is appropriate and what is not appropriate to give as a gift—the person would be unable to qualify as an example of generosity within the cultural group. The same sort of processes would apply to the idea of human examples as being examples of a future self. Cultural convention, along with structures of differentiation and similarity, work together to focus attention on the action of the example so that we see it as though we were doing the same things.

In sum, examples walk a line between similarity and difference; they are both deviants and conformists. They are tied to community history, standards, and ideals, while at the same time standing out as different from others within those communities. Our individual intentions and beliefs about what should be an example play only a limited role in what is eventually chosen as an example to learn from. To the that human examples function like other examples, then, the following conclusions can be drawn about human exemplarity:

1. Human exemplars become examples due to social conventions and to the placement of human beings within groups of other human beings.

2. A context of both strong similarity and salient difference within a group is often what makes exemplarity possible.

3. If a human being within a group becomes a particular sort of example, then it often has implications for what the other human beings can exemplify within the group.

EDUCATIONAL IMPLICATIONS

The analysis of examples and the process of exemplification casts doubt on the assumption of intentional exemplarity implicit in the standard model. The idea of an individual having control over who will serve as an example and how the learner will then interpret the example now seems naïve. This is not only because examples often refer to a more general body of constantly changing social meanings (i.e., to labels). In addition, it appears that larger social processes work to produce exemplification and these processes are always outside of any one person's control. This discussion of exemplarity has significant implications for education and suggests that what comes to be exemplified is largely beyond the power of teachers—the power of exemplarity instead derives from social groups. Examples always slip out of a teacher's hands, usually saying both more and less than what the teacher wants them to say.

This analysis shows that tutelary beliefs, the beliefs about someone else's desirable traits, are not sufficient if we want to understand how examples are selected. The context plays a central role is designating the people we notice as having desirable skills or personality traits and in unveiling these characteristics as future possibilities for ourselves. Beliefs also play a role, to be sure, but they must interact with social context. We might believe that all paintings possess the properties of viscosity, but this belief alone is not sufficient for any one painting to be an example of viscosity. In a similar fashion, a belief that a person has desirable qualities will not make that person an example of a future self. The example must speak in ways that communicate her qualities, and this communicative function is a result of the stage or context in which the example functions. Evaluative beliefs, then, about the desirability of certain human traits play a more limited role in learning by example than we might initially be tempted to think. The qualities of the model, and our beliefs about the model, by themselves do not create an example.

What this means is that teaching by example, in this sense, becomes a larger community project rather than one that can be limited to the intentions of individual teachers. Teaching by example is simply more than one person can handle. The social analysis of exemplarity, however, is still relevant to the task of the individual teacher. Even while we acknowledge these greater social forces, we can still say that the actions of the teacher (who can point out examples, give rewards for imitation, and so forth) form part of the student's social context. At least some of the factors involved with exemplification will be under a teacher's control, even though this control will be limited. The teacher can operate within social contexts that then serve to highlight and refine existing exemplarity relationships.

One thing a teacher can do within the limitations of exemplarity is to work to *create* a social group in which exemplification might take place. That is, the teacher can create a community of similarities and differences, which then serves as the basis of comparison and, therefore, of exemplification.[2] In essence, a teacher is able to do the same thing with human lives that I have done in this chapter with groups of squares, circles, and arrows. I have attempted to create comparison groups that have promoted the creation of specific examples. There is no reason to think that things would be different with representations of human lives.

This tactic of creating exemplarity by forming miniature social groups was often demonstrated in Classical pedagogical writings. Indeed, this is exactly what Plutarch does in his *Parallel Lives of Greeks and Romans,* perhaps the most famous work of biographical instruction ever written. Plutarch aims to use "history as a mirror," and he argues that, through comparison of parallel biographies, we are able to glimpse possible future selves. With this we are able to "fashion and adorn [our lives] in conformity to the virtues there depicted" ("Timoleon," 1). To this end, Plutarch creates groups of comparison by pulling together a series of Greek and Roman biographies and then using these groups to create the conditions necessary for human exemplification.

In Plutarch's first comparison of Theseus and Romulus, for instance, Theseus emerges as the clear example of human courage. The comparison works to create examples initially because of the similarity

Plutarch constructs between the two figures: They were both mythological heroes who were said to play key roles in the founding and
development of their respective cities (Theseus is the traditional founder
of Athens, Romulus of Rome). Although Plutarch finds similarity between Theseus and Romulus in that they were both ultimately failed
statesmen, he then reveals through narrative how they were clearly
different. Through this comparative work, Plutarch shows how
Theseus's deeds were usually bold, adventurous, and other regarding,
while Romulus was more timid and selfish. Concerning Theseus's
decision to confront the fearsome Minotaur, for example, Plutarch
writes, "[W]ords cannot depict such courage, magnanimity, righteous
zeal for the common good, or yearning for glory and virtue" ("Theseus
and Romulus," I, 4). Plutarch brings the stories of these two heroes
together in a context of both similarity and difference. In this way, he
creates the conditions necessary for heroic exemplification. Theseus
stands out as the example in the comparison group.

   This is not to say that Plutarch exercises complete control of
human exemplification. One could read these stories differently. And
our attention might also be drawn to other qualities of these Classical
figures due to the structures of similarity and difference that surround
us outside of Plutarch's context. A person who reads the story of
Romulus after having watched a biography of, say, Ronald Reagan
will make different connections of similarity and difference than the
ones Plutarch intended. Plutarch's comparison, then, is not the last
word, but his comparison does help to focus attention on certain traits
rather than others. Teachers have some power, even if ultimately the
power to teach by example escapes the individual's grasp.

   Another example of a writer using this comparative tactic to
create exemplification is the Classical satirist Lucian of Samosata. Like
Plutarch, Lucian creates small groups for the purposes of pedagogical
exemplification. He writes competing essays in which it is possible to
compare and contrast. Lucian is particularly interesting, though, because of the revisionist attitude that he takes toward the markers of
similarity and difference within his stories. One of his pedagogical
groupings consists of two philosophers and his purpose in the comparison is to exemplify the proper contemplative life. In his essay
"Demonax," which was mentioned in the previous chapter, Lucian
represents the life of Demonax as the proper exemplar of the philosophical life. He describes Demonax's freedom and liberty in speech
and action, and states that he was "straight, sane, and irreproachable"
in all that he did. His philosophy was "kind, gentle, and cheerful,"
and it made even the people he harshly criticized "better, happier, and

yes - teacher as interpreter - or a facilitator of SS interp's

more hopeful for the future" (Lucian, 1913 version, p. 149). To reinforce this judgment, Lucian repeatedly mentions the adulation Demonax received from the Athenians, whose magistrates arose in his honor when he came near and whose citizens lovingly attended his burial. The philosophers of Greece even reverently carried his body on their shoulders to his tomb.

Lucian contrasts Demonax with another philosopher named Peregrinus. In his day, Peregrinus was equally popular, but Lucian ridicules him and strives to reinterpret his life. In his essay, "On the Passing of Peregrinus," Lucian sets up a framework of comparison with Demonax by describing another sort of funeral, this time the funeral of Peregrinus. He tells how Peregrinus ended his own life by fire and shows that the high status hitherto accorded this philosopher's actions was undeserved. Lucian frames the death of Peregrinus as a pitiful act of a man obsessed with fame. He replays history to show Peregrinus as a devious manipulator only admired by the stupid and gullible. Unlike Demonax, he was admired by the "poor folk agape for largesse" (p. 19), that is, only by people who were easily manipulated (compare this to Demonax who was admired by magistrates and other philosophers). Although Lucian describes the funerals of both philosophers, he arranges things such that the adulation of Peregrinus seems undeserved.

Instead of being a Herculean act of courage, Peregrinus's suicide is interpreted as a shameful and useless grasp at fame. Thus, Lucian reinterprets not only the fame Peregrinus received as coming from fools, but also tries to reclassify the suicidal act itself. Lucian gives many reasons why the action should be reclassified. Lucian says that Peregrinus's fame was not deserved because his act was, in reality, cowardly and silly. His action is not something we would want children to imitate. If it really was a glorious act, he says, you would expect his followers to want to imitate it by killing themselves by fire, but they do not. The suicide would be admirable if done in the face of illness or suffering, but it was not. Finally, the suicide would have been done "decorously," Lucian claims, by enduring the heat in a motionless and stoic fashion, rather than by making a spectacle of himself, as Peregrinus did.[3]

It is vital to recognize what Lucian is doing when comparing Demonax and Peregrinus. The social markers, the markers of similarity and difference within a context, are being rethought and reapplied. The social markers that pointed at first to Demonax and Peregrinus equally (the fame and social adulation each received as they died), Lucian arranges through comparison to point only to Demonax. With this reinterpretation, Demonax stands out in the comparison group as

the rightful exemplar and proper model of imitation. Lucian is working within a system of similarity and difference to draw attention to
his favorite human example.

Lucian and Plutarch suggest how a teacher concerned with human exemplarity should operate. The teacher who wants to teach through
example should create a group whose differences highlight the desired
characteristics. The teacher should then work within the social markers,
and reinterpret them where necessary through the comparison, to facilitate the exemplification. In a sense, teaching with examples means participating in the preexisting social context. It is not simply selecting a
human being to be an example, it is about creating favorable conditions
so that the person actually comes to exemplify.

Let me repeat, though, that the preexisting social context places
limits on what the teacher may be able to arrange. A teacher may be
able to create exemplification groups within a certain context, but if
those exemplifications are not also reinforced outside of the classroom
walls they will be of limited pedagogical utility. If students remember
a teacher's example outside of school (which is what the teacher would
want), then new groups of comparison will emerge as they contemplate
the example in other social settings. The comparison group the teacher
constructs will never be the only group of comparison. The students
will take examples and form their own exemplification groups with the
resources presented by the larger community. This shows why exemplification must in the end be a community concern and why the community must be aware of the need for educational alignment. The teacher's
attempt to exemplify will always be partial and incomplete.

Even the larger community may face limits. The goal in education would be to arrange the community such that all comparison
groups point to exemplars that embody community values. If a teacher
tries to teach generosity through example, then the social markers
should be arranged in the larger community to support this example.
A perfect sort of alignment is probably impossible, though, and it is
not clear that we even know what such an alignment would look like.
Further, it is unclear whether such a complete alignment would be
ethically desirable. Should communities, after all, exercise strict control over the social markers that exist in the media and adult behavior? Should all institutions be transformed so that they create the
comparisons that convey the desirable characteristics through example?
Indeed, it may be that complete alignment of the processes of exemplarity with a moral or political consensus would be a dangerous
achievement. A totalitarian regime might align the processes of exemplarity so that such processes coincided perfectly with the values of

the regime, thus leaving little room for creativity or critical thought. Of course, this is not a problem unique to teaching by example. We might be equally concerned with *any* teaching endeavor that aligned perfectly with such a regime.

The deeper question is whether it is *possible* to align imitative exemplars with democratic values such as openness, critical thinking, and creativity. How can we teach creativity, while at the same time encouraging students to follow the examples of others? The imitation of exemplars, after all, can seem very uncritical, uncreative, and closed to the consideration of alternative possibilities. If a democratic community is serious about the educational importance of human lives, this is an issue that needs considerably more attention, and I will take it up in subsequent chapters.

One more word of caution should be sounded about exemplarity at this point. Harvey (2002) argues that examples become the frameworks for how we eventually come to see ourselves and understand our own experiences. I have pointed out that, since exemplarity often depends on differences within the social group, recognizing X as an example means that other members of the group are examples of not-X. Exemplification, then, is a way of building heterogeneous student grouping—something that clearly has political significance. If a person is acknowledged as exemplifying beauty within a group, then others by implication do not exemplify this trait. If a particular student is called out as being an example of a "hard worker," it also means that, within that group of students, the other students are examples of being "not hard workers." If a student is labeled as "gifted" in a school, the processes of exemplarity designate others as "not gifted." These examples are frames that influence how students see themselves and how they interpret their own experiences. When one student is framed one way, other students are simultaneously framed in the opposite way. A teacher might claim that, by pointing to a selected student, he or she does not necessarily mean to say anything about other students. But again, exemplarity transcends the teacher's intentions. Examples can crush as well as clarify, discourage as well as inspire.

CONCLUSION

In this chapter, I have begun to explore the assumptions of the historical tradition and have focused on the assumption of selection with regard to exemplars. Exemplarity is a significant pedagogical topic that intersects with larger social forces in many ways. Examples are particulars that, in some sense, represent generalities. The social character of human generalities (and labels that attach to human beings) ensures that exemplification always escapes our educational intentions and control. Human exemplarity occurs within social groups of both similarity and difference. Examples must be similar to the group in significant ways, while possessing differences that focus our attention on the exemplified features. This has important implications for education. Although the focus of educating with examples should be at the level of larger communities, educators can work to create groups of exemplification, rather than simply selecting isolated exemplars.

These points help us to understand some of the mysteries of exemplarity and imitation discussed in chapter 1. More will be said about these problems later, but for now a few quick points can be made. Consider first the medical school problem. Medical students intend that people-oriented physicians function as their normative exemplars, but in practice they often seem to adopt status-oriented physicians. This would indicate a failure in the process of alignment. The conventions and social markers of similarity and difference (status markers, salaries, and so forth) do not match up with ethical ideals. Exemplarity also relates to the problems of media violence. What determines how we "see" the violent act? It is not always what we might expect, because the processes of exemplarity are what determine the aspects of an action that we see. If we take Gavrilo Princip's violent action to be a "blow for Serbian nationalism," it will be because of the structures of similarity and difference surrounding the action, and, since our attention is drawn to those features, that action will then be the action we imitate (if we imitate at all). Notice that the imitation of this action could be expressed in nonviolent ways—perhaps in something like writing pro-Serbian tracts in a local paper, rather than assassinating political opponents. It is still imitation, to be sure, but of a different sort. An act of violence can be taken as part of a "future self" on many abstract levels, or it may be taken as an example of "not me," a self I do not want to become. It all depends on the context that surrounds the act of violence.

An example, then, mixes the singular with the normative. An example functions partially as an "induction," or as a particular that communicates something about a general. This Aristotelian understanding of an example has been the central topic of this chapter. But an example has also been thought of as something that serves as a standard, a prototype, or an ideal. This more Platonic understanding of examples has not yet been addressed. How is it that human examples go from communicating a trait to serving as a standard for that trait? How, in other words, do human examples go from telling us about a trait to calling us to adopt that trait? Why do some people become the standard that we follow?

CHAPTER 4

How Do Examples Bring Out Imitation?

We follow the example of some people and not others. The reason why has seemed obscure, even magical. Some people use the idea *charisma* to explain why a person inspires imitation—we want to imitate somebody else, it is said, because the person is charismatic. Charisma can be understood as an element of personal magnetism that allows its possessor to influence other people. It seems to involve an embodied combination of several characteristics, including persuasiveness, leadership ability, and physical attractiveness. The particular combination of traits involved with charisma, however, has been difficult to pinpoint—some good-looking people with strong personalities are not charismatic. Charisma has therefore often been considered a mystical gift coming from a divine source. In fact, the word is from the ancient Greek designating a "gift" or "grace."

Because the traits involved with charisma are so murky, it seems to say that a person "has charisma" is simply to say that the person has a particular effect on people. A charismatic, in other words, is one who inspires imitation and other disciplelike behavior. It is a description of the response of others rather than of a character trait (it is similar to claiming that someone is boring, which does not describe a particular set of characteristics so much as the effect of that person on others). We should not expect that the notion of charisma, then, will help much in determining what provokes imitation.

This old notion of charisma, however, does hold some clues to understanding imitation. For one thing, it teaches us how the imitative

53

response has often been viewed. We imitate, it has been assumed, because there is something special about the model. The particular qualities of the model attract others to that person with an almost gravitational force. At the same time, though, the invocation of charisma reveals the element of mystery involved with imitation. There is something about this personal attraction that seems to remain unexplained by describing the qualities of the model. Thus, the language of "gifts" and "divine grace" has been deemed appropriate. To have the trait of charisma, a person needs to be *given* something, endowed with a gift from the outside, to provoke this sort of powerful response. In what follows, I want to put a new spin on the nature of this "gift," and locate the source of grace at least partially within social contexts.

The question of this chapter, then, is why certain examples of human life become normative exemplars, that is, examples that bring out imitative action. I want to ask why some people (and some actions) provoke imitation while others do not. Obviously, not everyone we hold up as an example in a particular human endeavor inspires us to imitate. I can, for example, think of many people that I admire whom I do not find myself imitating. Charlie Parker is someone whose excellence in his particular endeavor (music) I have long admired, but I have never felt any inclination to imitate his example. He is an exemplar that I do not imitate. And it is not simply because I am not a saxophone player. There are other people who participate in practices that are foreign to me, and yet I still try to imitate or emulate these people, if only in abstract ways. There are also people within my arenas of practice whom I admire and consider good examples of the practice and, yet, do not find myself imitating. Success, excellence, and exemplarity by themselves, from my experience, are not sufficient conditions for an imitative response to occur.

When examining how motivation to imitate enters into human exemplarity, it becomes clear that there are several plausible ways in which it can be achieved. The standard model of how we learn from human exemplars, discussed in the second chapter, makes one assumption about how motivation enters into the exemplarity relationship. The standard model assumes consequential motivation, that is, it assumes that the motivation to imitate arises as observers see a model's action as having desirable consequences. The observers then imitate the actions that seem to lead to these desired consequences. Good perceived consequences will provoke an imitative response; bad consequences will not. Indeed, bad consequences might provoke the opposite action under this model, with the observer doing the opposite of what the model did.

What are we to make of this assumption? As I suggested earlier, this model does capture something about how certain forms of imitation seem to occur. When I am fishing and I see another person having more success than I am having, I will imitate the actions of that person. I learn the novel action, the use of a certain lure under certain conditions, by attending to the observed consequences. This explanation, though, is limited in its explanatory power. Imitation can appear spontaneously, without a conscious decision to imitate and without any reasonable connection to consequences we desire. Sometimes an action may even be imitated without any idea of the resulting consequences (think again of picking up an accent, a mannerism, or a turn of phrase).

So how else might we explain an imitative response? Early imitation theorists, such as Conwy Lloyd Morgan (1896) and Gabriel de Tarde (1903), suggested that imitation was an instinctual or constitutional tendency. We imitate, not because of a rational consideration of the consequences of an action, but because we are evolutionarily hardwired to imitate. With the sudden rise of the behaviorist revolution in psychology, however, these instinctual theories temporarily lost much of their popularity. In contrast to the instinctual explanations, behaviorists suggested that we are motivated to imitate certain people because of past reinforcement histories. We learn through imitation, to be sure, but first we must learn to imitate. For the early behaviorists, we learn to imitate because we have been rewarded for imitating in the past. In their classic book *Social Learning and Imitation* (1941), Neal Miller and John Dollard demonstrated that laboratory rats could be induced to increase their general imitative behavior by adding reinforcement after an initial imitative behavior. In essence, the behaviorist account reverses the assumption of consequential motivation: We imitate some people not because of the positive consequences we see them producing, as the standard model suggests, but because of the positive consequences that have been produced for us in the past through imitation.

The strength of the behaviorist account is that it seems to account for the nonrational component that is present with certain imitations. It is true that we often do not choose to imitate others; we simply find ourselves imitating. For the early behaviorists, imitation is not a means-to-end calculation to achieve a conscious goal; rather, we imitate because we have been conditioned to do so by our environment. The weakness of the behaviorist account, however, is connected to the limitations of behaviorism in general. It cannot explain adequately the production of novel imitations. After all, it seems common to imitate in new ways, ways that cannot be adequately explained through past reinforcement histories. We imitate people who were not present in our past, doing things that we have never been rewarded for imitating in the past. Further, the behaviorist account does not supply helpful explanations for specific instances of imitation. If we find ourselves imitating another and we ask the behaviorist why we are imitating, the behaviorist would say that *something* about our reinforcement history has triggered the imitation. But this seems more like an article of faith than anything else.

Another theory of motivation reaches back to the psychoanalytic idea of "identification." According to Freudian developmental theory, children are born with life-preservation instincts and sexual drives that require satisfaction. When a child attempts to satisfy a drive and is thwarted, he or she gains satisfaction by identifying with those who have had greater success. For example, male children begin to identify with their father because the father is able to have a sexual relationship with the mother (the male child's secret object of desire). The male child imitates the male parent and begins to associate himself with and replicate the actions of the parent as a way of satisfying otherwise unsatisfiable desires. Adults, for those influenced by this psychoanalytic tradition, continue to use identification as a defense mechanism against anxiety and frustrated desires. When our desires are personally thwarted, we are motivated to identify with those who are more successful, and this identification is manifest through imitation. Motivation to imitate is born from a desire to connect with others, rather than from a calculation to reproduce desirable consequences.[1]

One problem with the psychoanalytic approach to imitative action, of course, is the controversial theoretical baggage that comes with it (e.g., is there really this libidinous psychic energy that demands satisfaction?). And, as a theory of imitative action, it seems too limited. It fails in the same way the standard model does; that is, it does not explain the instances of imitation that seem trivial and unlikely to satisfy the expression of libidinal energy. Think about picking up somebody's particular turn of phrase. This often does not seem to have anything to do with identifying with someone who has a more satisfactory life. We do not always imitate people because we have a secret wish to participate, say, in their sexual exploits—they may not have any such exploits that seem desirable to us. Of course, the proponent of this view might simply say that we are repressing our desire and that is why we are therefore unable to recognize our true motivations. But this, again, is an article of faith and unsatisfying as a response. When we take the basic psychoanalytic idea, though, there are certainly elements of the theory that remain interesting. Imitation may indeed sometimes be a way of bringing an individual psychologically closer to the identity of another, and it is plausible to say that this

matching of identities may meet certain psychological or social
If so, then the satisfaction of these needs through identification may be
another mechanism that motivates an imitative response.

What is needed is a theory that fills in the explanatory gaps
present in these other theories of motivation. The theory needs to
explain the imitation that appears to be nonrational—that is, imitations that do not seem to be calculated to achieve some larger rational
end or to help us satisfy some forbidden desire. It also needs to recognize the novel nature of much imitation, that is, imitation of new
behaviors or imitation within new contexts. In what follows, I will
develop one proposal of how to look at imitation that explains some
of the instances of imitation that stand in need of explanation. The
theory builds on the work of William James and recent supporting
research in brain science and cognitive development. It does not so
much replace these earlier theories (or other theories of imitation in
psychology), but supplements them. Imitation in its various forms is
a complex phenomenon, to be sure, and multiple theories will probably be needed to fully explain it.

Note that the theory developed below is to be taken as suggestive
rather than final and comprehensive. I am certainly not a specialist in
each of the enormous areas of research that might prove to be relevant
(for example, the research in the cognitive sciences and neuroscience,
developmental psychology, social psychology, and so forth). While I
hope, of course, that the particular claims of the theory are useful, the
purposes of developing this theory are more (a) to suggest that assumptions of the educational tradition do not seem to account for all instances
of imitation, (b) to show what a possible alternative understanding of
imitation might look like, (c) to demonstrate how new understandings
of imitation could contribute to solving social problems, and (d) to illustrate how recent advances in empirical research might contribute to a
better understanding of how we learn from the lives of others. This
theory is not nearly as detailed as a comprehensive treatment would
need to be, but its purpose is more to point to possible alternative
avenues of understanding how imitation functions.

THE LINK BETWEEN ACTION AND PERCEPTION

William James and Ideomotor Action

Imitation arises out of a connection between the actions we perceive
coming from others and the actions we perform. The assumption of
consequential motivation assumes that, for an imitation to occur, the

perception of the action and the imitation of the action need to be connected through something called a "will" or a "motivation." In the standard model, this motivation is provided by a desire to obtain the observed
consequences of the action. The idea that actions and perceptions always need to be connected in this way by some third motivational
element, however, has been contested. One of the first to question the
necessity of this motivational element was William James in his *Principles of Psychology* (1890). In this text, James offers his famous account
of the "will" and develops his ideomotor theory of action.

When James looks at human action, he notices that there are many
different types of voluntary actions. It is true that some voluntary actions are preceded by enormous amounts of mental effort and conscious
decision making. We actively consider multiple alternative actions, weigh
their respective merits, and select the best choice. When we select the
best choice, we add a mental force to the idea, an act of will, and attempt to actualize the choice. A student deciding where to attend gradu-
ate school often seems to enact this sort of voluntary action.

James finds, though, that these cases are relatively rare. He points
to common examples from everyday experience. He writes of becoming conscious of dust on his sleeve and of simply finding himself
wiping the dust off his jacket. He does not weigh the merits of the
action and its alternatives. He does not feel that he summons an "act
of will" that motivates the action of wiping off the dirt. Sitting at the
dinner table, he finds himself taking nuts and raisins out of a dish and
eating them. He notes that he makes no mental resolve to perform
these actions and there is no extra feeling of being motivated. All that
he finds through introspection is the slightest perception of the object
and the transitory notion of the act. James argues that these more
automatic types of actions constitute the largest part of our daily actions. Many of our actions, he says, come about simply through the
introduction of an idea and not through an extra volition that adds
force to the idea we decide on among competing alternatives.

James develops the work of 19th-century psychologists such as
Lotze to argue that voluntary action consists of (a) the representation
of what is intended, and (b) the lack of any conflicting idea. The at-
tainment of both the idea and the lack of any opposing notion brings
forth the action. In James's words, "we think the act, and it is done"
(1890, p. 522). We have the idea of a light being on and, in the absence
of any conflicting idea, we perform the action of turning on the light.
Thus, James suggests that any mental representation is "in its very
nature impulsive" (1890, p. 526). He argues, "[E]very representation of
a movement awakens in some degree the actual movement which is

its object; and awakens it in a maximum degree whenever it is not kept from so doing by an antagonistic representation present simultaneously to the mind" (p. 526). Action and the perception of an action, then, are not distinct mental categories. Perception involves forming the idea of action that is already geared toward action, and the idea will be expressed in action unless there is another idea that impedes its expression.

Cognitive Science Research on the Action-Perception Link

Recent studies in neuroscience and developmental psychology seem to be proposing a similarly close connection between action and perception. Wolfgang Prinz has recently brought forward experimental evidence of "a functional role for similarity in the mediation between action and perception," which suggests, "action imitation is therefore a natural by-product of action perception" (2002, p. 160). Brain research also appears to indicate this link. Neuroscientists have discovered "mirror" neurons in the F5 area of the premotor cortex in the brains of macaque monkeys. The neurons fire *both* when an action is observed and when it is performed (Gallese, Fadiga, Fogassi, & Rizzolatti, 1996; Rizzolatti, Fadiga, Fogassi, & Gallese, 2002). In human brains, PET and fMRI studies have located common brain areas associated with both the perception and production of actions (Decety et al., 1997; Grèzes & Decety, 2001). Jean Decety's (2002) research suggests common neural regions involved in producing actions, perceiving actions, and thinking through actions (i.e., mentally simulating actions).

Vittorio Gallese and Alvin Goldman (1998) trace the implications of this research to the following conclusion: "Every time we are looking at someone performing an action, the same motor circuits that are recruited when we ourselves perform that action are concurrently activated" (1998, p. 495). They even go so far as to say that, when humans observe an action, they "generate a plan to do the same action, or an image of doing it themselves" (p. 499). If Gallese and Goldman are correct, then *any* idea of an action we gain through the perception of action is an idea of ourselves performing the very same action. All actions we perceive are mentally imitated even though the imitative response is sometimes inhibited and not played out in action.

There is also compelling research on an innate action-perception link in the developmental psychology literature and from clinical observations. Andrew Meltzoff's research (2002) suggests an innate perception-production linkage in human beings by showing that infants as young as 42 minutes after birth can imitate facial actions.

There seems to be an almost instinctual connection between at least some perceptions and actions. Somehow, newborn infants make what would appear to be a complicated connection between what they are seeing and their own actions.[2]

Additional evidence for an action-perception link comes from a wide variety of sources. Clinical investigators have noticed that some patients with prefrontal lesions in the brain are unable to inhibit their imitation of gestures or even some complex actions when they observe them (see Lhermitte, Pillon, & Serdaru, 1986)—a finding that parallels William James's observations on certain hypnotized individuals, whom he found similarly lacked an inhibitory response. The fact that perception automatically and involuntarily elicits actions in such circumstances suggests that actions and perceptions are closely related.

Still other studies in social cognition support a close connection and of action and perception. Some theorists in this area, for example, have demonstrated a strong "priming effect." Carver, Ganellen, Froming, and Chambers (1983) present evidence that suggests that if people perceive another person's hostile action in one situation, they are more likely to themselves produce a hostile reaction in situations that closely follow. In addition, the research of Bargh, Chen, and Burrows (1996) implies that observing another person's behavior increases the likelihood that the observer will replicate the same behavior—a finding supported by subsequent studies (Chartrand & Bargh, 1999). They call this the "chameleon effect." There are various theoretical explanations for this, but the empirical finding is well established: Seeing another's action often prompts us to do the same action. This is exactly what a theory of action-perception linkage would predict.

The convergence of all this evidence suggests that James was right. On a very basic level, action and perception are not necessarily separate faculties that always need to be connected through something called "motivation" or an "act of will"; rather, action and perception are built on the same mental foundation. As I watch somebody doing something, there is evidence to suggest that I simultaneously and automatically think of myself doing the same action. There is, at least sometimes, no extra step connecting the actions of another to my own actions. The perceptions of an action, on a basic level, have already become *my* action. The key question in imitation, then, is not why some actions we perceive motivate imitative action; rather, the question is why we do not imitate all the actions we perceive. Or, as Prinz writes, "[T]he problem is not so much to account for the ubiquitous occurrence of imitation, but rather for its notorious nonoccurrence in many situations" (2002, p. 16). James and Prinz, then, would both argue that this whole question of finding out how examples motivate us to replicate an action is the wrong starting point—we should instead ask why some examples *do not* compel us to action.

THE SENSE OF SELF AND THE
IMITATIVE SORTING MECHANISM

Impulsive Ideas Interact with Our Sense of Self

If all ideas are inherently impulsive, but only some ideas are acted upon, there must be some sort of process that inhibits some of the impulsive ideas. There must be something that sorts out the impulsive ideas that are unleashed in action and those that are inhibited. But how does this sorting process occur? James thought that what prevented a representation of an action from actually awakening the action was the simultaneous presence of "an antagonistic representation" (1962, p. 692). In short, an idea brings about a corresponding action unless there is a different idea competing with it for attentional resources. We imitate unless there is a rival idea that interrupts our focus on the action. If there is a sorting mechanism, then, it probably lies in the shifting focus of attention. We might have a headache, or be worried about bills, or be thinking of a lover—all of these may shift our attention away from the impulsive ideas that would otherwise be expressed in imitative action.

There is more to say about the sorting mechanism when we consider how attention might be connected to the relatively omnipresent ideas relating to who we are. Indeed, if we were to ask about the common sources of the antagonistic representations that inhibit the expression of impulsive ideas, it seems that one of the most likely candidates is the *self*. After all, the idea of action we gain from perceiving others will always coexist with our ideas of who we are, and it makes sense to suppose that the selection of the ideas to be imitated would appear to have much to do with the person we consider ourselves to be. As I perceive the bowl of peanuts on the table, the idea of peanuts coexists with ideas about myself, about my known passion for peanuts, and about my concerns relating to health and weight gain. My ideas about myself would be a constant source of "antagonistic representations" (or, indeed, of supportive representations). Any perceived actions, and the impulsive ideas I form from such perceptions, will always be interacting with ideas about who I am as an acting agent.

Evidence that imitative responses interact with our sense of self is supplied by the research of Ap Dijksterhuis (2005), who suggests that the automatic imitative response interacts with what he calls our "self-focus." He accepts that imitation is our default behavior: We imitate unless something happens to impede the imitation. His research involves priming some research participants with readings that involve certain stereotypes (stereotypes of politicians or professors) while other participants do not receive such priming. The participants are then asked to perform certain tasks, such as writing an essay. Dijksterhuis found that those participants who were primed performed their assigned tasks in ways that agreed more with the stereotype than those who were not primed. People who were exposed to the stereotypes of "long-winded French politicians," for example, imitated the stereotype by writing longer essays. Most important for our purposes, however, was what happened in the condition that placed research participants in front of mirrors to perform their assignments. In this condition, the imitation of the stereotype disappeared. This suggests that imitation is automatic only when people remain focused on the stereotype and not on themselves. The self is, or can be, an antagonistic representation that distracts us from the actions we perceive. Before examining more closely this relationship between self, others, and imitation, then, we should probably consider the question of what the "self" actually is. This might be the first step in understanding the nature of the relationship.

The Nature of the Self: Self and Narrative

One of the most promising theories of selfhood that has been raised, especially in the latter half of the 20th century, is the idea of a narrative self. In a highly influential paper published in 1992, Daniel Dennett argues that the self is not a thing or substance; it is, rather, more like a "center of gravity." A center of gravity has a certain reality, to be sure, but not because it is an object we can point to—it is not a physical reality. Rather, a center of gravity has a reality within a system of explanation. It is indispensable in some areas of explanation. We simply could not fully explain why a chair falls over without this idea, or at least an idea that is similar. For Dennett, the self is also an explanatory reality. It is the center of a system of stories that involve an individual as the main character. In making sense of our lives, we could not do without it. The self is the center of gravity among the stories we tell about ourselves. The self is founded on narrative. Other prominent philosophers who endorse the idea of the narrative self include

Charles Taylor, Alasdair MacIntyre, and Paul Ricouer (although they differ in the details of their accounts).

Philosophical arguments for the narrative self are largely conceptual. What we refer to when we use the word "self" is a collection of meanings about who we are. Meanings, it seems, are largely created through stories. We might be able to have certain experiences and possess certain memories, but those experiences and memories do not have meaning until they are placed in the form of a narrative. If I pick up a ringing phone and hear a voice telling me, "The bluebird flies at midnight," that event has no meaning without a story around it. Through stories, we construct meanings about who we are, we connect to each other and to our environment, and we draw a sense of where we are going. If meaning is created through stories, and if the self is a collection of meanings, then the self would seem to be constituted through storytelling.

The idea that the self is constructed through the stories we tell about ourselves has gained a degree of empirical support, in addition to being theorized by philosophers. John Bickle, professor of philosophy and neuroscience, has reviewed PET-scan research and found that, during moments of quiet inner speech (when we talk to ourselves inside our own heads), the areas involved with both language production *and* comprehension are active. Thus, human beings simultaneously produce and comprehend their own speech acts. We do not just speak to make ourselves understood to others, he suggests, but to understand ourselves. He cautiously suggests that this PET finding "yields empirical evidence for a narrative concept of self" (2003, p. 198).[3]

Bickle is not alone, however, in thinking that he has found empirical support for the idea of a narrative self. In a much different sort of project, Lawrence Langer (2003) has examined oral and written histories of Holocaust survivors and has produced evidence showing that stories of survival are infused with the narrative theme of a "missed destiny of death," which subsequently affects the survivor's subsequent sense of self. Further, Fivush and Buckner (2003) have presented evidence suggesting that early narrative engagements with parents make a demonstrable impact on a child's subsequent gender identity. Therefore, the idea that the self is constructed through narrative makes sense conceptually and has a degree of empirical support.

Positing a narrative self does not necessarily mean that we have comprehensive and unified life stories that we consciously refer to for guidance and meaning. Indeed, some people may feel that their lives are simply a string of disconnected episodes. Philosopher Galen Strawson has this in mind when he writes, "I have absolutely no sense of my life as a narrative form, or indeed as a narrative without form. Absolutely none" (2004, p. 433). He does not feel that there is a story connecting his past self to his current self in any meaningful way. He doubts many people have grand, comprehensive narratives that tie together the disparate moments of their lives.

Strawson is probably right about the common lack of experience of an explicit, fully unified, and conscious life narration. He does not, however, deal with the accumulated evidence in favor of the narrative conception of the self and his own account is inconsistent. In explaining his life as a series of disconnected episodes, Strawson weaves something of a story in its own right, as do the authors he uses to support his point. His account of himself is a very real story; indeed, it is the story of not having a story. It seems hard to believe, furthermore, even for one committed to living in the moment, that it would be possible to navigate the world without at least a partially coherent sense of how the past influences the future. It would be impossible to explain the force of promise keeping in our lives without some sort of narrative, however consciously undeveloped that story may be. Our act of keeping a promise is only meaningful with a story of ourselves that includes a past event—the making of the promise. Strawson writes, "Well, if someone says, as some do, that making coffee is a narrative that involves Narrativity, because you have to think ahead, do things in the right order, and so on, and that everyday life involves such narratives, then I take the claim to be trivial" (p. 439). The charge of triviality here does not come from any inherently trivial nature of basing current action on a coherence of past experience and future plans. It simply derives from the trivial example of making coffee. Substitute "making coffee" with "making a wedding vow," and it is clear how nontrivial the process he describes becomes. Anytime we explain the nature of our actions, we almost always construct something like a story to give our actions meaning.

Strawson is correct, though, in his doubts about people conceptualizing their lives as one ethical-historical-characteriological narrative. It is more likely that we have various scattered narratives that, although we must sometimes determine how these subnarratives hang loosely together, it may be a far cry from a comprehensive, unified story in which all the pieces of our lives fit together nicely. Most of us probably have multiple narratives, for example, that find expression at different times. We do not have to see our lives as being a unified quest where all the elements find a comfortable narrative role, but we do have to reconcile the subnarratives somehow when we think about who we are and what we ought to be doing. A loose sense of self (of

Post-hoc?

selves), being comprised largely by a series of partial., subnarratives, is all that is required for narrative to retain a ce.. psychological importance in human life.

We appear to be justified, then, in positing that the self is deeply constructed by stories—stories that are constructed by individuals within communities. There are conceptual and empirical arguments to support the idea that our sense of self consists largely of the stories that we tell about ourselves. Through storytelling conventions—plot, characterization, theme, and so forth—the experiences of life take on meaning and continuity. Narratives draw together disparate memories, bind them with emotion, and produce meaning.

THE NARRATIVE-SELF THEORY OF IMITATION

Constructing the Theory

So far, I have developed the following ideas: First, all ideas of action, including those ideas gained from perceiving the actions of others, are *inherently* impulsive. Second, not all ideas are acted upon, so there must be a process that inhibits some of the impulsive ideas. Third, our sense of self would be one important factor in this inhibition, because the ideas of actions will coexist with ideas about who we think we are. Fourth, the self is fundamentally constructed on autobiographic narratives that involve evaluative elements. From these elements, it is possible to construct a theoretical framework for how representations of human life bring about an imitative response.

To construct this framework, we would first need to ask about the possible relationships between the perceived action and the narrative sense of self. We can frame these relationships in terms of congruency. The process of imitation involves perceiving another person's action, and a perception of action (according to recent research) involves formulating the idea of myself doing the same action. This mental simulation of myself doing the perceived action may or may not be congruent with my narrative conception of self. Indeed, there are at least three possibile ways in which the perceived action may be related to the narrative self: (a) A perceived action of another can form a *positive congruence* with a narrative self; that is, the action is congruent with who I consider myself to be. (b) A perceived action of another can form a *neutral congruence* with respect to the self; that is, the perceived action may be indifferent to who I consider myself to be. And (c) a perceived action of another can form a *negative congruence* with the narrative self; that is, the action may run contrary to who I consider myself to be.

A theory of imitation that takes seriously the link between action and perception may be formulated around these different modes of congruence. Initially, the theory could be stated as:

> (T1) An already impulsive idea is unleashed in imitation if the idea is congruent with ideas originating from my narrative sense of self.

As stated, this theory would offer some explanation of why all ideas do not automatically bring forth an action. Note, though, that this formulation is too vague: Does it mean that there must be a positive congruence between the narrative self and the perceived idea? The prominence of seemingly trivial instances of imitation, which other theories of imitation do not successfully deal with, implies that the inhibitor needs to be less selective. Simply put, it cannot inhibit everything that lacks a positive connection to the self because many actions that are imitated do not seem to have anything to do with a narrative sense of self—I do not imitate that turn of phrase because it connects with my narrative self (at least not in any obvious way).

These questions lead to the following reformulation of the theory of imitation:

> (T2) Those examples of human action that provoke imitation are those that are *not incompatible* with the narrative sense of self.

Under this formulation, the only impulsive ideas that are inhibited by the narrative self are those that have a negative congruence. If the idea is neutral with regard to the narrative self, or if there is a positive congruence, then the impulsive idea will be unleashed in action. The narrative self only inhibits impulsive actions that are fundamentally opposed to the self-identity constructed by central life narratives. Those ideas of human actions are brought out in action when they are not inconsistent with the stories we tell about ourselves and about our place within our communities. Notice the negative wording here of being "not inconsistent." The theory is framed in this negative way because it reflects the Jamesian idea of the already impulsive nature of ideas. The theory is not so much an attempt to explain imitative responses per se since that does not need an explanation, at least not at the level I am concerned with. Rather, the theory is an attempt to explain why we do not imitate some impulsive ideas.

This theory is promising because it deals with the nonrational side of imitation, something that the standard model of imitation does not account for. It seems that we do not often make conscious decisions to imitate in order to achieve some consequence. Instead, we simply find ourselves imitating. Sometimes we never recognize the fact that we are imitating; at other times, we only realize we are imitating after a long time has passed. The narrative self theory of imitation shows how this nonrational imitation happens (ideas are already infused with imitative energy), but it also explains why not all actions are imitated. They theory also accounts for instances of novel and trivial imitation that the standard model, the behavioral model, and the psychoanalytic model fail to deal with successfully. We imitate trivial actions, actions that are not connected to larger goals, past reinforcement histories, or libidinal objects of desire because ideas are inherently impulsive and they are only inhibited by antagonist representations.

This theory relates to some common beliefs about how human examples function. For instance, one of the arguments for affirmative action in higher education is based on a role-model theory, which says that students from underrepresented minority groups need people that are "like them" to serve as models. According to this theory, students are better able to imitate those who share their characteristics and backgrounds than those who do not—a notion that is supported, to some degree, in the literature (see, for example, Ashworth & Evans, 2001; Evans, 1992; Klopfenstein, 2002; Link & Link, 1999; Rask & Bailey, 2002; Zirkel, 2002).[4] The benefits of a matching background are explained by the theory as it is formulated. People that come from the same backgrounds and communities are more likely to find elements of congruence in the narrative self and the modeled actions are thus less likely to conflict with the impulsive ideas. Similarity in background means that an imitative response is more likely to be forthcoming.

Of course, the functioning of actual imitation would be a complex business. Not all actions may easily be classified as consistent, not consistent, or neutral with respect to the narrative self. Some actions, for example, may be partially consistent and partially not consistent or neutral. The scope of the imitation in such cases depends, perhaps, on the relative salience of the different aspects of the observed actions. If I see somebody pushing another out of the way of an oncoming car, it matters how I classify the various aspects of the action I see. "Pushing an innocent bystander" may be rejected as being incompatible with my sense of self and therefore inhibited. "Saving a life" may be deemed compatible and brought forth in action at an appropriate time. The aspect of the action that commands the most attention is likely to be the action that is imitated.

This example of saving the life brings up another way in which the execution of the action is a complicated affair. In addition to depending on the conceptualization of the action that is perceived, the imitative action also seems to depend on certain enabling conditions. I may see a person saving another's life by pushing the person out of the way of the oncoming car. This action may be compatible with my sense of self, that is, it may be an action that is not rejected by who I consider myself to be. If there is not a pedestrian threatened by a speeding car, though, <u>I would be</u> unable to imitate the action.

Furthermore, according to research on the action-perception link, it is not just the mechanics of motion that comprise the representation of the already impulsive action. Rather, the goals and tools play a part in the idea, as well. The experiments with macaque monkeys show that F5 neurons are "correlated with specific hand and mouth motor acts and not with the execution of individual movements like contractions of individual muscle groups. What makes a movement into a motor act is the presence of a goal" (Gallese & Goldman, 1998, p. 493). Thus, many grasping neurons only increase activity when the monkey observes a hand trying to take possession of an object, rather than simply viewing the hand going through the muscle contractions involved in grasping something. Although no similar phenomenon has yet been observed in human beings on the neuronal level, there is some evidence that we also structure our perceptions of actions in terms of goals. Meltzoff has shown that even eighteen-month-old children can "see through" the physical mechanics of an action to the action's intended consequences. For example, in one experiment an adult was observed throwing something at a target, yet always missing. It turned out that the observing child did not imitate the action of missing the target, even though this is only action that had been observed. Instead, the child tried to hit the target. Meltzoff concludes that even very young children understand the goals implied by unsuccessful attempts (2002, p. 32). Likewise, Gattis, Bekkering, and Wohlschläger (2002) present evidence showing that children understand the actions that are being modeled, and select what is important to imitate, by trying to understand the goals of the action. In their view, "[I]mitation occurs through a goal-sensitive mapping between observed actions and performed action" (p. 201). We perceive actions, then, in a way that is oriented around the goals we perceive the action to aim at. Perception of action does not reduce simply to representations of physically manifest behaviors.

What this research seems to suggest is that if I see a person using a screwdriver, it is not the case that my idea of "the action" would

perceived

consist in a certain twisting motion of my right hand. The idea would also include the purposes of the action and the tool used in the action. Thus, in order for an imitation to arise from the already impulsive idea, the possibility of a goal would also have to be present, as would the availability of the means to accomplish that goal. That is to say, the impulsive idea needs enabling conditions that would allow both for the action to be performed and for the goal to be realistically achieved.

Consequence?

In response to the complexities of imitation, then, the theory of narrative imitation should be reformulated as:

> (T3) Those perceptions of human action that provoke imitation are those that, all things considered, are classified such that the action is not incompatible with the narrative self and that exist within an enabling context that allows the imitation to take place.

?

The new phrase about classification is necessary to respond to the complex nature of perceived actions—actions we observe are not always simply compatible, neutral, or incompatible with our narrative self, but instead are often mixtures of these designations. The phrase dealing with enabling conditions reinforces the centrality of context in allowing for the actual execution of the already impulsive perception.

The Narrative Self and Imitation: Some Objections

More would need to be said about many aspects of this theory, for example, about what sort of structural relation would need to exist between the mechanics of the impulsive ideas (perhaps based in mirror neurons) and of the narrative self. For now, I can only explore three further questions: (a) Does the idea of the narrative self as a sorting mechanism square with the phenomenology of an imitative response? (b) Is this type of sorting mechanism compatible with what we know about psychology and neuroscience? And (c) what are we to make of cases where imitation takes place but that seem to go against a narrative identity? As we answer these questions, it is important to remember the proposed scope of this narrative-self theory of imitation. Although it may subsume some aspects of the other theories at times, it is only intended to help us understand some kinds of imitative action, not all kinds of imitative action. These three questions will help us test the limits of this sort of theory and better grasp what it can and cannot explain.

From a phenomenological perspective, it does not seem accurate to say that an explicit process of narrative reasoning occurs before all imitation. As James pointed out, we seem to think the thought and then automatically perform it. We do not have an idea of an action, consider its place in our core life narratives, and then perform it if we find the action not incongruent with our life narratives. This is especially true for the imitation of simple behaviors and mannerisms—it would be odd to think that a yawn induced by somebody else's yawn occurred because, upon reflection, it was deemed as being "not inconsistent" with existing life narratives. Indeed, when we see an action performed, we usually do not rehearse in our minds our autobiographical narratives and then decide from these narratives whether the action converges with our stories. It would be just as implausible to say that all imitative action comes at the end of a process of explicit storytelling as it would be to say that all imitative action comes at the end of means-to-end analysis, as in the standard model.

From the perspective of neuropsychology, it also appears to be wrong to say that imitation follows a process of explicit inner storytelling, at least as far as storytelling is performed via inner speech. Bickle's studies (2003), although they support the idea of a narrative self, also seem to indicate that the verbal, storytelling regions of the brain have little contact with the parts of the brain involved with action formulation. He concludes that the narrative self usually functions only to understand past action, rather than to formulate future action. The language production and comprehension centers, the parts of the brain presumably essential to a narrative self, are too far removed from the parts of brain involved with action perception and execution. This seems to suggest that action production (and therefore imitation) has no connection to explicit narration.

The first thing to say in response to these objections is to point to research that does appear to find a link between action formulation and the verbal regions of the brain. The mirror neurons described earlier have been found in the monkey homologue of part of Broca's area. Mirror neurons are those neurons that manifest the link between perception and action. Further, it has been found that Broca's area is active when human beings imitate (Iacoboni, Woods, Brass, Bekkering, Mazziotta, & Rizzolatti, 1999). This is important because Broca's area is also one of the central language production and comprehension areas (focusing on syntactical comprehension). Thus, it appears that some language production and comprehension areas in the brain are linked with some areas of the brain involved with action formulation—indeed, with regard to certain forms of imitative action, the language and action areas appear to be precisely the same.

This is a long way from showing, of course, that a process of storytelling is involved with the formulation of imitative action. And from the perspective of phenomenology, it still seems as though we do not usually narrate in any sense before imitating actions. We think the thought, as James said, and it is done. In response to this sort of phenomenological objection, it appears more clarity is needed about how the narrative self might influence imitative action. When we look at the relationship between self, narrative, and action in consciousness, it may be more accurate to say that life narratives work to construct a *sense* of self, and it is this sense of self that matters in action formulation and imitation. The storytelling process has already done its job, so to speak, by constructing this "sense" or "feeling" of who we are. Autobiographical narratives are still playing an important role in sorting imitative responses, then, but they do so by creating a feeling of self that inhibits actions rather than by a process of narrative reasoning inhibiting the actions directly. If we allow for this type of mediation between narrative, observation, and action, we can retain the explanatory power offered through the narrative self while not offending phenomenological or neuroscientific evidence.

One way to understand how autobiographical narratives influence the sense of self is to think of William James's description of the stream of consciousness. Consciousness is a flow of ideas that blend into one another. An idea is influenced by what has gone before and it subsequently influences what comes after it. "For an identical sensation to recur," James writes, "it would have to occur the second time in an unmodified brain" (1890/1967, p. 28). Since the brain is always modified by sensation, one never has the same idea twice. When we hear a sudden burst of thunder, we are not only presented with the idea of thunder, but thunder preceded by silence: "Into the awareness of the thunder itself the awareness of the previous silence creeps and continues; for what we hear when the thunder crashes is not thunder pure, but thunder-breaking-upon-silence-and-contrasting-with-it" (p. 34). Even though an idea is not immediately present in consciousness, its effects remain. So it is with any idea: Its appearance in our minds is influenced by what has gone before, and it, in turn, influences what comes after. What this means for the relationship between narrative and the self is clear. Even though a life narrative is not immediately present in consciousness, its effects linger on and influence what comes later.

But is it even too strong to say that an imitative response is usually based on a congruence with a background sense or feeling of self? Take the example of the yawn. It still does not seem plausible to suppose that an imitated yawn is a convergence between an action and background sense of self. That is, there still appears to be a wide range of imitated actions that have nothing to do with even an ephemeral, narratively constructed sense of self. Some might also claim that the narrative-self theory of imitation cannot account for very early imitative responses. As I have pointed out, Meltzoff's research (2002) suggests innate imitative responses by showing that infants as young as 42 minutes after birth can imitate facial actions. Surely, infants this young have not developed a narrative sense of self.

I grant all these points, which is why the initial theory was so carefully worded. The theory was stated in negative terms. An imitation will proceed whenever an already impulsive idea does not *conflict* with a narrative sense of self. This is very different from saying that an imitative action is manifest whenever there is a positive connection between an idea and the narrative sense of self (although positive connections may also occur). Our sense of self, constructed through autobiographical narratives, may have nothing to do with many actions we observe. If I consult my narrative sense of self, for instance, I would not consider yawning to be a relevant issue. Since the yawn does not conflict with my sense of self, the idea's impulsivity is unleashed in action. It is not the case, though, that yawning is an important element of my sense of self and that I imitate the yawn because there is such a connection. Many actions simply have no bearing on our sense of selves and are not subject to imitative inhibition.

Another objection relates to the times when we imitate actions that seem counter to our sense of self. Don't we sometimes seem to imitate actions when conscious reflection would reject the actions as being incompatible with our values? Imagine a young man from a very conservative and very proper household who joins the Navy, and before long, imitates his companions' use of salty language. Finding himself imitating in this way, the young man feels like he has violated his core values. If imitation is based on a background sense of self, how would such a thing be possible? If, in fact, there are unconscious imitations such as these that go directly against someone's sense of self, then this would count as evidence against this type of theory. I would argue, though, that this judgment should not be made too hastily. It is important to recognize that we usually tell many stories about ourselves and there is nothing to ensure that the stories are fully consistent. Nor is there anything to ensure that we will imitate positive examples, since we also sometimes tell negative stories about ourselves. Usually, we tell both positive and negative stories about who we are. The self, as was pointed out earlier, is not a unitary, internally consistent entity.

It may therefore be better to say that impulsive ideas interact with our *senses* of self rather than from a unitary sense of self. The young man may have a narrative in his mind (that he may not even want to acknowledge) that allows for the imitation of objectionable actions. Or, indeed, another model of imitation may be appropriate in such cases (he may see his companions gain rewards from tough language; if so, the case would fall under the proper purview of the standard model). Whatever the solution, such cases would indeed make the analysis of imitation more complex. But they would not necessarily provide a refutation for the narrative-self theory of imitation. Narrative may still play an important role even in cases such as these. Taking these objections into account, however, seems to require a further reformulation of the theory of imitation. The final reformulation emphasizes the nonunitary nature of the narrative self:

> (T4) Those perceptions of human action that provoke imitation are those that are classified in a way so as to be not incompatible with the narrative *senses* of self and that exist within an enabling context that allows the imitation to take place.

As it stands, there may be several ways of testing this sort of theory. When and if sufficient neuroscientific evidence accumulates about the self, this theory would predict some sort of relationship among the parts of the brain dealing with imitation and the parts dealing with self-understandings and narrativity. It may also be possible to test in social laboratories and field work by acquiring an in-depth understanding of individuals' narrative identities and looking to see if there is a relationship between these identities and subsequent imitations.

THE SOCIAL NATURE OF NARRATIVE AND IMITATION

In the above sections, I have suggested that the sense of self—constructed largely through autobiographical narrative—inhibits or facilitates the imitation of already impulsive perceptions. This suggestion implies that imitation and imitative learning have a deeply social nature. Narrative, after all, is a social phenomenon; it is not produced solely within an individual mind. If narrative constitutes the self, and if the self is playing a role in mediating the imitative response, then the imitative response is also a social phenomenon. It is a participant in its social milieu. If educators want to understand how imitative learning occurs, then they may need to look to broader cultural and historical concerns.

The first social influence on narrative, and also on the narrative self, is the influence of language. By language, I mean not only spoken or written language, but any system of signs present within the social context (e.g., a wink). The influence of language on stories can be seen even when we consider a referential view of language, which sees language as simply a way of naming things. The stories people tell are limited by the names and signs by which they can categorize the world. Language, however, does more than simply refer. It has many different functions: joking, solemnizing, promising, criticizing, and so forth. Such functions are intimately tied to specific cultural activities or language games. Stories that make use of language must tie back to cultural activities to gain meaning. It would be impossible to formulate a meaningful story in isolation from the activities and practices of a cultural group.

Perhaps it is for this reason that bilingual speakers often feel a deep change in the self as a result of being immersed in a new language. A new language entails a shift in cultural perspective. Ervin's (1964) early work with French-English bilinguals found that such individuals highlighted different cultural themes on the Thematic Apperception Test (TAT) depending on the language they were asked to use. Schrauf and Rubin (2003) summarize current research and autobiographical accounts of second-language learners and write:

> For these individuals, more poignantly, immigration and second language learning brought with them a sense of profound loss of the mother tongue and "mother culture" and their replacement or substitution by the adopted culture. For these authors, the shift in language brought with it a corresponding shift in identity. (p. 123)

One reason for this deep shift in identity is that language is deeply tied to cultural activities. It is not just how we talk about things, it is how we connect with groups and institutions. Language shapes our narratives and this shapes how we think about ourselves.

The second way in which the social world connects to narrative is through the narrative conventions that exist within a particular culture. This is probably just a subcategory of "language," but it is important enough to be considered on its own. Stories are almost always developed and narrated according to the cultural conventions of a good story. In Western societies, at least, stories usually include a context, a problem to be solved, an attempt by a protagonist to solve the problem, and a relation of the consequences (Mandler & Johnson, 1977). Fivush (1991) points out that personal narratives often do not involve a problem to be resolved. "But even in a personal narrative," she writes, "one must provide the setting or orienting information.

Moreover, personal narratives usually involve some kind of internal reaction" (p. 61). The effect of such narrative structures is to channel our attention to certain features of experience and away from others.

Narrative conventions are not universal and they differ, at least somewhat, among cultures. It has been argued that this has a demonstrable effect on memory and self-concept. Leichtman, Wang, and Pillemer (2003) have studied autobiographical storytelling among Chinese, Korean, Indian, and North American adults and children, and found that differences in storytelling practices were associated with the cultural emphasis of "independence" versus "interdependence." Those individuals who were raised in "independent" societies, the authors claim, told stories that were longer and more elaborate, and had to do with earlier memories than those in "interdependent" societies. They go on to argue that culture influences autobiographic narrative because of different beliefs relating to self-construal, emotions, and a personal past. If such studies are accurate, then it seems that differences in cultural belief along these dimensions change storytelling practices, and with them, the construction of the narrative selves. In other words, our cultural storytelling conventions change how we come to think about ourselves. The self, again, is inextricably social.

The next factor that influences the construction of narratives is the audience that the narrative is directed toward. The philosopher Jonathan Glover has argued that our autobiographical narratives are partially created through social interaction. When we talk with others, the audience often plays a significant role in helping us to construct and tell our stories. The audience shapes our stories as well as hearing them; indeed, we often do not have fully formed stories until we try to express them to others. "In this way," Glover argues, "we can share in the telling of each other's inner story, and so share in creating ourselves and each other" (1988, p. 155).

Audience changes our stories in various ways. We usually tell stories with an audience in mind and we try to anticipate how they will react to elements within our stories. We tailor stories to match the audience—we deemphasize or omit some elements and highlight others, we offer contextual details to justify controversial decisions, we draw analogies to other stories and situations our audience is familiar with. Storytelling comes with purposes and agendas, and we change stories so that we can accomplish our goals with the audience. The type of audience—a social fact—changes the fundamental nature of our narratives.

The influence of an audience is manifest not only when we are standing in front of an audience. Audience also exerts power when we tell ourselves stories about ourselves. As we privately narrate who we are, we are always mindful of what others would think of the story we are weaving. As Jerome Bruner writes:

> Telling others about oneself is, then, no simple matter; it depends on what *we* think *they* think we ought to be like. Nor do such calculations end when we come to telling ourselves about ourselves. Our own self-making narratives soon come to reflect what we think others expect us to be like. (2003, p. 211)

Through the social expectations manifest in inner narrative, our self-concept becomes part of a public domain. The audience matters, whether the audience is real or imagined, friendly or hostile. The audience changes, in short, the character of stories we tell. Since audiences influence how we tell our stories they also change our identity, and this, in turn, will influence who we come to imitate.

Discussing audiences in this way, however, is incomplete because it treats storytelling as a set of skills that are already in place before they are brought in front of audiences. In reality, however, storytelling skills are created *from* interaction with audiences. Early conversations with parents, especially mothers, seem to be particularly important to a child's developing self. Developmental psychologist Robyn Fivush's work has been significant in showing how the developmental process plays out. Using a longitudinal analysis, Fivush presents data showing strong correlations between a mother's narrative elaboration and the later storytelling ability of her children. She argues, "[T]he ways in which mothers structure conversations about past events early in development are related to children's subsequent abilities to structure personal narratives" (1991, p. 59). Fivush would later posit, "Both mothers and fathers were significantly more likely to use an elaborative style when talking about the past with daughters than with sons" (1994, p. 143). Not only does this result in the finding that "girls remembered significantly more information about past events than boys did" (p. 143), but also in a different self-concept for girls. Since parents talk more about the past with girls and do it with more social embellishment and emotion, girls become more attuned and connected to the emotional lives of others. Of course, one does not have to fully accept this particular story of gender development to see how storytelling differences in early childhood might affect later self-concepts. The people with whom we engage in storytelling activities are not just a passive audience that we move through our stories; rather, from the beginning, other people are playing an active role in shaping how we develop the basic skills and attitudes of storytelling, and this, in turn, affects self-concept. The amount of storytelling that our social world encourages may itself be a factor in who we later become.

In this section, I have outlined some ways in which the social world influences the construction of personal narratives. Language, storytelling conventions, audiences, and other social interactions all work to shape these supposedly "personal" stories. Since personal narratives largely constitute our sense of self, any change in personal narratives also influences our self-concept. Changing aspects of narrative will not only influence our current self-concept, but will also influence our ideas of a future self and, consequently, it will end up influencing who we imitate. Any changes in the social context of narrative will, it seems to me, also shape the imitative response. The imitative response is dependent on communities and social groups. Just as with the processes of exemplification described in the previous chapter, the imitative response does not reduce to an isolated observer watching and deciding to imitate a model.

EDUCATIONAL IMPLICATIONS

We have seen that theories of how an example inspires imitation each contain certain limitations. It was therefore necessary to construct a new theory that cohered with phenomenological experience and psychological research. James was one of the first to observe that "motivation" is often unnecessary in a description of how actions occur. Action and perception are intimately linked; ideas often call forth action without an additional act of will. But if ideas are inherently impulsive, then the question becomes why all ideas of action are not imitated. When considering this question, it became clear that there must be some type of sorting process. A promising candidate for this sorting mechanism, I have argued, involves the narrative sense of self, which inhibits those impulsive ideas that are inconsistent with its content and structure. If this sorting process is indeed grounded in a narrative sense of self (and we have some reasons for supposing it is), then the imitative response is not always under the control of the individual. It is dependent on social structures, conventions, and histories.

The next question is, simply, so what? What difference does it make to look at human exemplars and their influence in this way? To understand why this might be important, consider the problem of objectionable human examples in education. By this, I mean the question of how we handle situations when we see that people are imitating models we would consider inadequate, immoral, or harmful, or when we fear that they might do so. This is one of the central concerns in the debate about violence in the media. A large portion of the censorship debate has to do with concerns about modeling and imitation. If children are exposed to violent role models, we worry that children will imitate these models and thereby acquire violent, immoral, or reckless tendencies.

Unfortunately, there is evidence to support such fears. The classic work is Albert Bandura and colleagues' laboratory research on aggression (1961, 1963), which shows that children do imitate the violent actions they observe in others. The effect of violence in media has received growing support since Bandura's initial explorations (for a recent assessment, see Huesmann, 2005). A sensible reaction to this problem is to censor those representations of human life that are violent or cruel. In this spirit, library materials are carefully screened, internet connections taken away or aggressively filtered, and so forth. If we grant such power to imitation, censorship seems to be the only acceptable response. It seems even more acceptable if we grant the link between action and perception endorsed earlier—every act of violence children perceive instigates a process of mental simulation in which the children execute the action they observe.

This justifiable impulse to protect children and adolescents from violent or unethical models, however, conflicts with another justifiable impulse in liberal democratic societies to grant to individuals a robust freedom of expression, even to those who might say or portray things that are troubling or unwelcome.[6] The impulse to censor objectionable models also conflicts with certain educational goals, since representations of troubling human life can be profoundly educational. A film with bloody television images from the Vietnam War, say, might combine extreme violence with important educational material. Even violent entertainment can contain important educational content (perhaps Spielberg's film *Saving Private Ryan* or Kubrick's *A Clockwork Orange* are examples). Often the censor's brush paints too broadly, covering over the challenging and educational material along with the objectionable material—indeed, they are often the very same thing. Finally, censorship is often ineffective. Children find ways to access such material, in spite of efforts to censor. How do we navigate these real concerns about censorship with our equally valid concerns about the imitative impact of violent media?

The theory of imitation developed here suggests a different way of looking at the causes of imitative learning. Imitation of objectionable models, under this analysis, does indeed proceed because the child observes a model. The existence of the model is a necessary condition, but it is not a sufficient condition. According to the narrative self-theory of imitation, the idea of the modeled action must also be deemed as "not inconsistent" with the narrative sense of self for imitation to actually occur. Imitative action requires both the existence of a model and also a certain relationship between the idea of the observed action and the narrative sense of self.

This requirement has significant practical implications. If we are worried about negative role models producing a troubling imitative response, then, there are two areas of action. We can act either on the existence or visibility of the model, or we can act on the narrative selves that come into contact with the model. Since the first solution conflicts with freedom of expression or other educational concerns, it seems that the second solution is preferable. Instead of acting to eliminate the existence of bad models, the focus of attention should be on the stories that come to constitute the narrative self. The goal would be to have the narrative self label as "inconsistent" a violent, immoral, or unsafe representation of human action. By engaging with a child's underlying narratives, it would be possible to prepare the child for exposure to the objectionable models that they will almost certainly encounter in a free society. It is a sort of inoculation through engagement with narrative identity.

There is some initial evidence that suggests this approach would be effective. One study (Huesmann, Eron, Klein, Brice, & Fischer, 1983) used an educational program to reduce the amount of aggression in grade school students. The experimental treatment involved helping the students take ownership of the idea of nonviolence. For example, the students composed essays explaining why television violence was not like real life and why it was bad to imitate such violence. The students were videotaped and then watched themselves reading the essays as a group. Later, the students who were exposed to this treatment were significantly less likely to be rated as aggressive by fellow students than were students in a control group. Their beliefs about violence had also changed. The researchers describe their results in this way:

> The final level of aggression was lowest and the attitude change was the greatest for children who initially had identified less with TV characters. Also, the greatest reductions in aggression were

obtained for children in the experimental group who both im-
proved their attitudes and reduced their identification with TV
characters. (p. 908)

The relationship between the violent images and self-identity seems to
be central to understanding this reduction in aggression. The children
came to identify themselves less with the violence they were exposed
to, and were thus less likely to imitate the violence. It is likely that,
through the experimental treatment, the stories that the students were
telling about themselves had shifted. They remembered seeing themselves reading the antiaggression essays. Afterward, violence formed
an antagonistic idea that was more likely to be rejected by the self.

Engaging with the narrative self would be possible in several other
ways. The first thing to be done would be to encourage children to have
experiences that, for example, do not involve solving problems through
violence. But after undergoing such situations, students should be encouraged to tell stories about their encounters and to integrate their
experiences with their larger life narratives. Care should be taken in
how the stories are told. The meaning of the stories that are told will
depend on social factors that can be used to promote a nonviolent sense
of self. From the research reviewed in the pervious section, it seems that
the meaning of narratives depends on: (a) the storytelling conventions
that shape the stories, that influence how characters behave, and that
point to the elements that comprise a meaningful narrative, (b) the
audiences that are exposed to the narrative, and (c) the early narrative
interactions that lead to storytelling skills and attitudes.

It is important the children have experiences with nonviolence,
experiences that will form the narratives that contribute to the sense
of self. It is equally important, though, that these experiences are
meaningfully framed in the ways listed above. Storytelling conventions can vary, for example, in how much they focus on individual
actors or communities. A narrative approach that emphasizes the larger
community context of action would form part of a narrative identity
that more affectively rejects violent and other socially destructive
models. The meaning of our life narratives also changes depending on
the audiences that hear our stories. If we tell our stories in front of
audiences that value nonviolence, we are likely to emphasize this aspect
in narrative and our identities will then have a more prominent aspect
of nonviolence. Finally, Fivush might argue for a narrative approach
with young children that fosters a rich storytelling interaction and
emphasizes a concern for the feelings and needs of others. It might

also emphasize a concern for those affected by our actions. Any of these three approaches may work to help an observer resist the beckoning presence of a violent example. Violent actions can still be portrayed and given expression in a free society, and the way is still open to learn from depictions of violence, if necessary. But the force of the model to inspire imitation will have been defused.[7]

Three caveats should be added to this narrative-self approach to objectionable models. First, this type of response can go only so far. Very young children probably do not possess rich self-narratives, and thus the narrative self as an imitative sorting mechanism will probably be inoperative. Imitation, for young children, is probably dependent on other considerations. For such children, then, some other sort of protection from adverse models seems appropriate.

Second, repeated exposure to models of a particular sort can change the sense of self. Our sense of self influences who we interact with, to be sure, but who we interact with also influences the narrative sense of self. If I am constantly exposed to violent or cruel people, then this will probably begin to affect the stories I tell about myself. Theorists of narrative point out that the self is dynamic. The self is always changing because life stories are always changing. One warning that should accompany the narrative response to imitative violence, then, is that the narrative self is continually shaped and reformulated. In other words, it is incorrect to think that there is a static group of stories that create a forever unchanging sense of self. The stories themselves change by what we come into contact with. So the process of narrative storytelling must be continually renewed rather than seen as eternally immune from violent models.

Finally, there exist additional processes of imitative learning other than the impulsive model I have been addressing. The standard model of imitation, for example, is still operative in some cases, especially for higher-level types of imitation. It does seem to explain certain imitations. If the consequences of violent action are significantly attractive, then the processing of imitation occurs on another level—a level on which calculative deliberation, motivation, and will come into play.

Even with these considerations it seems that this approach to thinking about imitative violence is preferable to solving the problem through censorship. When thinking about media violence, the narrative-self theory of imitation reveals that there may be alternatives to simply limiting children's exposure to bad models. Thus, how we think about the imitative response matters in important questions of public policy.

CONCLUSION

This chapter has developed a narrative-self theory of imitation, which describes imitation as being largely (but not entirely) determined by the nature of the congruence between a narrative identity and an already impulsive idea. A lack of contradiction between the narrative self and the impulsive ideas will elicit an imitation, provided there are no other competing ideas present. If we say that the self is one primary inhibitor of impulsive ideas, however, it seems we are also committed to recognizing a strong element of social influence in the imitative response. The theory is suggestive rather than comprehensive, but it does point to possible understandings of imitation that are different from the assumptions of the standard model, particularly with its strong emphasis on consequential motivation.

If we were to outline the process of imitative action completely, we would begin with the notion of exemplarity presented in the previous chapter and then move to the narrative-self theory of imitation. Through structures of similarity and difference within social contexts, our attention is drawn to some people as examples. We come to perceive them in certain ways. The idea of action that exists in these perceptions is already impulsive, and it will be unleashed in action unless there is a competing idea. One important source of these competing ideas is often our narrative sense of self.

So what, then, is the relationship between exemplarity and imitation? On one level, exemplarity plays a role in imitation by mediating the perception of actions. On another level, though, it could be said that exemplarity mediates how we perceive ourselves. It structures who we think we are and the autobiographical narratives we construct. After all, our own autobiographical narratives are also based on examples drawn from experience. Our sense of example will help construct our personal stories, and our stories will then influence the examples we see and imitate. Exemplarity, perception, and the narrative self are involved in an intricate dance that is consummated as one life influences another.

CHAPTER 5

The Social Meanings of Imitation

As a new parent, I would often find myself imitating my infant daughter. She would make burbling noises and I would follow. She would throw up her arms and I would do the same. She would stick out her tongue and so would I. As I participated in this (some would say) undignified activity, I found myself asking why my daughter and I played this imitation game. The complete answer is probably complicated and obscure, but one thing I noticed was that such actions built, in my mind at least, a certain bond between us. I felt closer to her as we imitated each other. It was as if we had formed our own little community, and through these primitive imitative responses, we had begun to construct a common way of life. The imitative action, in other words, had a certain meaning; it was a way for us to communicate and show interest in each other.[1]

In this chapter, I develop the idea that the repetition of an action is fraught with social meanings that cannot be ignored if we want to understand how exemplars function in influencing human lives. The point of this discussion about meanings is ultimately to address the question of the value of imitative learning, which will occupy the last chapters of the book. In examining the role of imitation in education, I will not be the first to highlight the centrality of imitative meaning. That the repetition of an action has meaning was noticed by Søren Kierkegaard, for example, who asks several pertinent questions in the voice of Constantine Constantius:

As for the significance which repetition has in a given case, much can be said without incurring the charge of repetition. When in his time Professor Ussing made an address before the 28th of May Association and something in it met with disapprobation, what then did the professor do? Being at the period always resolute and *gewaltig*, he pounded the table and said, "I repeat it." So on that occasion his opinion was that what he had said gained by repetition. A few years ago I heard a parson deliver on two successive Sundays exactly the same discourse. If he had been of the opinion of the professor, as he ascended the pulpit on the second occasion he would have pounded the desk and said, "I repeat what I said last Sunday." This he did not do, and he gave no hint of it. He was not of Professor Ussing's opinion—and who knows if the professor himself be still of the opinion that it was an advantage to his discourse to be repeated again? At a court reception when the Queen had told a story, and all the courtiers laughed, including a deaf minister, who then arose and craved permission to tell his story—and told the same one—the question is, what was his view of the significance of repetition? When a school teacher says in class, "I repeat that Jaspersen must sit still," and the same Jaspersen gets a bad mark for repeated disturbance, the significance of the repetition is exactly opposite. (1843/1946, pp. 135–36)

In this passage, Kierkegaard rightly notes the complexity involved with the meanings of repetition in action. The meanings attached to repetition, in each of the cases above, seem to fluctuate according to the particulars involved with each case, that is, according to the whos, whats, whys, and hows of the repetition. The repetition has meaning, to be sure, but it is a meaning that is difficult, if not impossible, to specify apart from immediate contexts. Even in specific contexts the meaning of repetition may be contested.

Imitation is a particular case of repetition that usually involves a person repeating (if even abstractly) the actions or attitudes presented by somebody else. Imitative repetition presents many different meanings. Sometimes imitation is taken as a sign of respect for the person who is imitated, even of worship as in the notion of imitating God, *imitatio dei*. Sometimes imitation is taken as an act of plagiarism, sometimes as an act of mockery, sometimes as an act of conformity. Sometimes the meaning of imitation may go even deeper. It may, as Nadel and colleagues write, be a "way to evoke an abstract object or person to make the past be present via pantomime: for example by facial expression, bodily evocations of events and emotions connected with events" (1999, p. 209). Indeed, imitation is never meaningless. When I repeat what somebody else does, it is an act of communication in the social world. Imitation that serves a communicative function has sometimes been called "mimesis" (from the Greek word for imitation, *mimeisthai*).

It is my contention that the meanings involved with imitation shape all social environments and perhaps most prominently educational environments. The educational significance of imitation resides not only in what an observer may learn from watching and repeating an action, but also in the meanings such actions produce and the relationships these meanings create. Exemplars may be learned from, in other words, but they may also create the environment within which learning takes place.

This point is suggested by examples from the historical tradition. Consider the following educational advice from Isocrates to the young student Demonicus:

> Pattern after the character of kings, and follow closely in their ways. For you will thus be thought to approve them and emulate them, and as a result you will have greater esteem in the eyes of the multitude and a surer hold on the favour of royalty. Obey the laws which have been laid down by kings, but consider their manner of life your highest law. For just as one who is a citizen in a democracy must pay court to the multitude, so also one who lives under a monarchy should revere the king. ("To Demonicus," 36)

Notice that Isocrates advises the imitation of kings partly because of the action's communicative qualities, that is, because of the meaning that imitative action conveys. His advice to follow the pattern of kings is not simply intended to provide helpful information about successful kingly behaviors. Isocrates takes imitation to also constitute a particular message from the imitator, in this case, a message that the imitator endorses the royal models ("you will thus be thought to approve [the kings]"). In addition, Isocrates seems to believe that patterning one's life after the royalty alerts people to the attempt at imitation itself ("you will thus be thought . . . to emulate [the kings]"). The imitation points beyond itself to the adoption of a broader range of actions on the part of the imitator, even extending to imitations that have not yet been observed. Thus, Demonicus's repetition will be taken to imply that he approves of the current regime and also that he has adopted their larger ways of life as his own. In these ways, Isocrates thought, imitation creates an environment in which a person can be initiated into desirable activities.

Perhaps the most interesting feature of this passage is that Isocrates sees imitation as a tool of social influence. A result of the imitation will be a "greater esteem in the eyes of the multitude and a surer hold on the favour of royalty." The people who observe Demonicus's imitation will increase in their affection for him. Most important, the royalty, seeing the imitation, will be more likely to grant favors to Demonicus. Isocrates thus suspects that imitation has certain meanings that can produce favorable responses both in the person being imitated and in outside observers. For Isocrates, the social meanings attached to imitation (the communicative aspects of imitation) were inseparable from understanding the educational functioning of imitation. The royal models would show Demonicus how to act like royalty, to be sure, but the imitation of these models would also work to advance Demonicus's upward social trajectory. It would open doors to new practices.

Recent studies in developmental psychology have also suggested that imitation is not only "an important mechanism of social learning in human culture, but also a powerful means of signaling interest in another person, used for purposes of communication" (Dautenhahn & Nehaniv, 2002b, p. 20). The majority of the recent empirical studies examining imitation as a means of communication have involved infants and toddlers. Many developmental theorists argue that infants are able to have a social presence through imitation that would otherwise be unavailable until the achievement of language. Infant imitation has been seen as a central means of communication and as a vital step in eventually developing more advanced ways of interacting (Nadel et al., 1999). It allows young children to communicate as they imitate and are imitated. Ina Uzgiris has argued that imitation should be seen as a form of shared social engagement. Imitations may "serve to establish a mutually constructed, shared world between the participants and to bring the culturally constituted world known to the adult into the infant's experience" (1999, p. 192). Although some theorists think that imitative communication is abandoned with the development of language, as I will soon point out, there are studies that strongly imply that it continues into adulthood.

This chapter will examine the meanings involved with imitative activity and how those meanings influence educational environments. To better grasp the meanings involved with imitation and exemplarity, it will be necessary to examine some common reactions to imitation and then to extract the possible meanings of the imitation implied by these reactions. These reactions can be found in statements from philosophy of education and have also been documented in empirical studies about how people respond to being imitated. Beginning in the late 1950s, in fact, social psychologists have observed a complex array of reactions to an imitative act. Thus, there are plenty of studies available for inspection on this point, and it seems reasonable to attempt to understand the meanings of imitation implied by these documented reactions to imitation. This is will be the central methodological approach I will use to tackle the problem of imitative meaning.

As an example of my approach, consider the work of social psychologist Mark Thelen (1981) and colleagues, who report that children often enjoy being imitated, particularly when they are unsure of themselves. In these circumstances, imitation is said to "reinforce" the behavior of a child model—if a teacher imitates the student, then the student's performance of the imitated action will increase. However, at least with some developmentally challenged children, imitation of student behavior (a teacher sticking out her tongue in imitation of the student) led to a reduction of the students' behavior (the students' own tongue protrusions decreased) (see Kauffman, Hallahan, & Ianna, 1977; Kauffman, Hallahan, Haas, Brame, & Boren, 1978; and Kauffman, Snell, and Hallahan, 1976). From these different reactions to being imitated, it seems reasonable on the most general level to conclude that imitation can possess both positive and negative meanings within a social context. Apparently, in some circumstances, imitation has a meaning that makes a model uncomfortable with his or her actions; in other circumstances, the meaning of imitation can produce an opposite, more positive reaction.

THE MEANINGS OF FOLLOWING AN EXAMPLE

Imitation is often taken to say something about somebody else. It might reveal the social status of the model or, at the very least, might show what the imitator thinks of the model. As I imitate, I can be seen, by myself and others, as offering a judgment and expressing my opinion about the model. Imitation can be a commentary, offered by the imitator, on the worth and status of the person who is imitated. It seems fairly obvious that the person who is imitated can take meaning from the imitation—imitation, after all, is said to be the highest form of flattery. The person who is imitating, however, may also find meaning in the imitative act, as in the case of my imitation of my infant daughter. The imitation meant something to me as an imitator. Finally, in addition to being meaningful for both the model and the imitator, imitation may also be significant to observing third parties. Notice that in the Isocrates passage discussed earlier, the meanings surrounding imitation are taken to extend both to the model (the king) and to others who are observing (the people). The fact that the model is being imitated says something about the model to interested bystanders. Imitative action, for Isocrates, can be a meaningful statement about the model to the imitator, to the models themselves, and to third parties looking on.

Imitative Meanings Related to the Model

The meanings that imitation may communicate about the model vary enormously across different contexts. Imitation may, first of all, be taken to communicate something positive about the model. Imitation is often seen as a recognition and acknowledgment of status, skill, or experience. It is an act that conveys respect, even reverence. Once we understand imitation as a signal of respect, the empirical research is not at all surprising. People tend to generally prefer those who imitate them more than those who do not (e.g., Dabbs, 1969; Kauffman, Kneedler, Gamache, Hallahan, & Ball, 1977; Lesser and Abselson, 1959). If imitation is taken as an acknowledgment of competence and expertise, we would expect people to react favorably to it—and, indeed, people often do. Imitation may be a commendation, a pat on the back.

The positive message sent by imitation is strong enough that it can play the role of flattery (something, again, that Isocrates seemed to realize). Indeed, imitation can often be an effective way to ingratiate oneself and gain social influence. Thelen and colleagues summarize the benefits that can come to the imitator:

> [T]he literature suggests that being imitated is reinforcing; that it leads to increased attraction toward the imitator, increased imitation, increased reward to the imitator, and evaluations of the imitator as better adjusted, more likely to succeed, and more desirable for future interaction. Clearly, the effects of being imitated described above are positive effects, the kinds of reactions that people often solicit (in one way or another) in their interpersonal relationships. Since these effects can be obtained by imitating, it is a reasonable inference that people may imitate in order to influence the behavior of the model; that is, people may imitate as a proactive attempt to deal effectively with their social environment. (1981, p. 410)

Thelen supports the inference that imitation can be a tool of social influence by pointing to a wide range of studies. One study showed that children who were classified as "leaders" were, paradoxically, more likely to imitate others than those who were classified as "nonleaders" (Dollinger & Thelen, 1978). In another study, children were told they would get a reward if they could get another child to respond to their requests during a game. "When given the opportunity to imitate," Thelen and his colleagues write of the experiment, "the children who were motivated to influence imitated the other child more than the children in the control condition" (1981, p. 411). They also point to research on conformity in social psychology, which suggests that matching another's actions is a way to gain approval and rewards. Although most of these studies are now decades old, the conclusion has also been supported by more recent research. One experiment, for example, found that waitresses who mimicked the way their customers placed their orders received larger tips than those who did not (van Baaren, Holland, Steenaert, & van Knippenberg, 2003).

One could say, then, that at least in some circumstances, imitation is a way to get people to like you and to get them to do what you want them to do. Specifically, if you want people to do what you are doing, you should first imitate them. It is a powerful way to manipulate others. With this in mind, Thelen rightly concludes that imitation is not necessarily a passive, thoughtless reaction to an environment (as, for example, the Enlightenment thinkers often feared). Instead, it can be an active way to shape an environment according to one's wishes—it is, or can be, an expression of human power. The positive meanings involved with imitation can be tools of social influence. Imitation seems to operate as a form of flattery, by sending a positive message to the model from the imitator.[2]

So far, I have concentrated on the possibilities of imitative meaning that cast the model in a favorable light. Sometimes, however, imitation can have the opposite meaning. It is well known that, in some classrooms, students mimic teachers as a sign of denigration and disrespect (and teachers mimic students for similar purposes). Imitation can be a way of mocking behavior that is perceived as annoying, idiosyncratic, or strange. It can suggest a *lack* of respect for the model, and thus can have meanings quite the opposite from what I have argued above. Thus, it makes sense that, in some circumstances, studies have shown imitation leading to a decrease in a modeled action (such as the studies with tongue protrusions described earlier). One thing that remains constant, though, is this: Imitative meanings can be a tool to actively engage and modify the social world. If I mockingly imitate you to get you to stop doing something, I am hardly being passive.

The meaning of the imitative act, therefore, can reflect at least two different types of things about the model. It can be a sign of respect for the model or it can be sign of denigration of the model. Some have pointed to even deeper meanings of imitation. For the model, imitation has sometimes had the significance of being a "mirror," which presents the model with an occasion to examine her actions as seen through the eyes of an outsider. In the Classical world, Plutarch thought this reflective function of imitation could create an important educational opportunity. For Plutarch, the mirror reflected both ways. The parent should be an example to the children, and should thus reflect back to children an image of the children's future selves. But, in addition, parents can also see themselves in a new way as the child begins to imitate them:

> Fathers ought above all, by not misbehaving and by doing as they ought to do, to make themselves a manifest example to their children, so that the latter, by looking at their fathers' lives as at a mirror, may be deterred from disgraceful deeds and words. For those who are themselves involved in the same errors as those for which they rebuke their erring sons, unwittingly accuse themselves in their sons' name. If the life they lead is wholly bad, they are not free to admonish even their slaves, let alone their sons. Besides, they are likely to become counselors and instructors to their sons in their wrongdoing. ("The Education of Children," 14A)

The imitating child is taken as a reflection of the model. If the child acts wrongly, the parents should correct themselves as if they were seeing their own reflection misbehaving in a mirror. In this way, imitative meaning becomes a vehicle for self-knowledge.

Imitative Meanings Related to the Action

Just as imitation says something about how the model is regarded, it may also function as a signal of attitudes and opinions regarding the particular action that is modeled. In some circumstances, if I am imitating a model, it seems to be a sign of approval of the observed action. It is a way of giving applause, a nod of approval, or a thumbs-up to the action that the model undertakes. Indeed, in his *Emile*, Rousseau uses imitation as a way of approving of Emile's action. Rousseau writes, "In the morning let Emile run barefoot in all seasons, in his room, on the stairs, in the garden. Far from reproaching him, I shall imitate him" (1762/1979, p. 139). Emile's delight in the natural world is not to be diminished, but nourished, and this is to be encouraged by teacher imitation.

On a still deeper note, the early Nietzsche seems to use imitation as a way of validating life; or, at least, of validating the passionate life of the Greeks. In *The Birth of Tragedy*, Nietzsche uses imitation of human beings as a kind of life-affirming theodicy—a justification for human pain and suffering. He argues that the Greeks were "keenly aware of the terrors and horrors of existence; in order to be able to live at all they had to place before them the shining fantasy of the Olympians." To meet the challenges of their existence, the Greeks erected a conception of divinity: "The gods justified human life by living it themselves—the only satisfactory theodicy ever invented" (1872/1993, p. 34). The Greeks invented gods who imitate humanity, Nietzsche argues, to justify human existence in a world of misery and pain. Imitation by the gods is a vindication, not of any particular action, but of Greek life generally.

Imitative Meanings Related to the Imitator

In addition to expressing something about the model and the action, imitation can also say something about the person who is imitating. If I imitate somebody, I send a message about myself to the model and perhaps to others who may be observing. The fact that I am imitating may be taken to reveal something about my willingness to be shaped by those around me. That is, it may be taken to say something about my desire to conform or my teachability, my humility or subservience. When I imitate, I often suggest an openness to being molded, touched, or manipulated by those around me. Perhaps this is why imitative behavior often increases the ease of social interactions. Tanya Chartrand and John Bargh (1999) have demonstrated, for example, that when research confederates displayed mimicking behavior they were generally thought to be more likable and easier to interact with than when they that did not mimic. Imitating the actions of another person, even the speech and postures, can send a message that we are open to the other person, that we are listening, and that we are responding to his or her presence.

In addition to sending a message of openness to others, Plutarch argues that looking at our own tendency to imitate others is one way of gauging the progress of our moral development. In his essay in the *Moralia*, "Progress in Virtue," he writes that people should not only commend and admire what is praiseworthy, but emulate the action as well. The extent of one's desire to imitate praiseworthy action is a way to test one's development of virtue.

> We must therefore believe we are making but little progress so
> long as the admiration which we feel for successful men remains
> inert within us and does not of its own self stir us to imitation. In
> fact, love for a person is not active unless there is some jealousy
> with it, nor is that commendation of virtue ardent and efficacious
> which does not prod and prick us, and create in us not envy but
> an emulation over honourable things which strives earnestly for
> satisfaction. (84 B–E)

For Plutarch, then, the desire to imitate is meaningful as a measure of
personal virtue. Admiration of a virtuous person, without a corresponding urge to replicate that person's virtue, is a sign that something is
amiss in the development of morality. This is another way in which
Plutarch develops the idea of imitation as a mirror and as a moment for
self-reflection. The engagement with a human exemplar through imitation is, again, seen as an opportunity to increase self-knowledge.

Inquiring further into the meaning imitation has as it relates to
the imitator reveals that an imitation can suggest something about the
nature of an imitator's relationship with the model. In its most extreme form, imitation may reveal an imitator's desire to be unified
with the model. In religious traditions, the act of imitating a divine
figure can be an act of worship or an act that expresses loyalty to a
faith tradition. Divine imitation is not simply a way of acting in the
world so as to curry divine favor (although it may certainly be that,
too). The imitative act is also a sign that the imitator desires a certain
sort of relationship.[3] As John Barton puts the matter in his study of the
Hebrew Bible, the ethics of imitation is "not so much [about] a system
of obligations as a way of communion with God" (1998, p. 130). Imitation, in this case, reveals the hopes and desires of a community as
it seeks union with the divine.

Recent commentators on the ethics of the Hebrew Bible find
imitation to be meaningful in various ways. Harry Nasuti (1986) points
out that, in the Pentateuch, readers are commanded to identify both
with the captive Hebrews in Egypt and with the God who eventually
sets them free. Thus, the author of Deuteronomy writes, "[God] loves
the sojourner, giving him food and clothing. Love the sojourner, therefore; for you were sojourners in the land of Egypt" (Deut. 10:18–19).
Later the author implores generosity to newly freed slaves, "As the
LORD your God has blessed you, you shall give to him" (Deut. 15:14).
In a complex web of meanings, then, Israel is told to identify with the
oppressed who were blessed by God, while at the same time identifying and imitating the God who was the agent of liberation. The reader

of the Pentateuchal law is urged to affirm connection to both communities through imitative actions and their associated meanings.

Overall, imitation can be a way of both sending and receiving social feedback. As such, it is a form of communication involved with satisfying the human need for recognition—the need to be seen by others as we see ourselves, and to be liked and respected in the social world. Through imitation we send the message that we recognize, admire, and are fond of another person or action. Through imitation, we are also presented with a mirror to examine ourselves as others see us. We are able to step outside ourselves and watch our actions performed by somebody else. Through imitation, we are recognized as being part of a group or designated an outsider. As we imitate, we can be seen as affirming or denying a connection to those around us. Imitation is, in these ways, central to the formation of community.

IMITATION AND COMMUNITY IDENTITY

This relationship between imitation, recognition, and community should be of particular concern to educators. At least since John Dewey began discussing the idea of "developmental democracy" in education—the notion that participation in democratic units fosters the development of human potential—one of the central questions of modern education has been how individual students can grow to become contributing members of cooperative communities. One of the most important reasons why these imitative meanings matter is precisely because of how such meanings construct and maintain these communities. Imitative meaning should therefore be a topic of interest to teachers and administrators who want to foster the development of educational communities. Imitation is not the only factor mediating community membership and identity, but it plays a central role.

Of course, on one level it seems obvious that imitation mediates group membership. If nothing else, imitation seems to indicate which groups we are a part of because it creates a degree of behavioral uniformity within groups. This is partly the impulse behind uniforms in the military, schools, or athletic teams—it marks off members of a group as distinctive. In this regard, there is nothing mysterious about the social functioning of imitation. Even with this acknowledgment, though, we may still be underestimating the influence of imitation. Group mediation through imitation often occurs unconsciously and can be enacted on many different levels.

One way imitation covertly mediates community identity is through the positive social reactions that are often achieved through imitative meanings. As I have already indicated, there is widespread agreement among psychologists that, at least under certain conditions, imitation is linked to liking, affinity, and empathy and that it facilitates interpersonal bonding and collective action. Imitation, then, often simply promotes prosocial sentiments. It casts the imitating individuals in a favorable light and it increases the likelihood of reciprocal imitation in the future. With these positive social reactions, it is likely that imitative action will help to produce viable social groups.

The aspects of imitation that build community, however, extend far beyond building a prosocial sentiment. Indeed, it seems that imitation plays a part in *temporally mediating community membership*. That is, the repetition of actions and attitudes through imitation shapes and reshapes our conceptions of the groups we belong to along a continuum of time. Imitation changes our past, present, and future views of our relationships to particular groups. Further, imitation specifies not only the boundaries of group membership, but also the terms of membership. Imitation reveals not only what groups I belong to, but also what group membership means.

Imitative Mediation of Past Conceptions of Group Membership

When I say that imitation mediates past community membership, I am not making the simple (but true) claim that we feel a part of the groups whose members we have imitated in the past. It is not simply that I feel part of a team because I have previously imitated the members of the team. Rather, I am making a more Heideggerian claim about the openness and indeterminacy of the meanings we attach to the past. Our actions in the present, and the people we imitate in the present, change our understandings of the past. The past is as full of real possibility, in this sense, as is the future. The past is not merely a set of possibilities that have come to pass, have ended, and are now no longer possibilities. If the past continues to exist in the present as significant events to which we attach meaning, then, as the present moment changes, the significance of the past will also change. As present-day art historians find new significance in past works, for example, the past is shown to remain open. The meaning of the past changes; it will never disclose all of its possibilities.

The new significance we come to attach to past events is related to how present imitation mediates the past with respect to community

sense of self → how what how likely we are to imitate

membership. One of the most important ways in which present imitation changes the significance of the past is through the imitation of storytelling practices within a group. Imitation of storytelling allows people to see their past lives as uniting under similar interpretative patterns. As a novice imitatively adopts the storytelling practices of her group, she begins to see her past in ways that coincide with membership within the storytelling community.

Psychologists Jean Lave and Etienne Wenger, looking at ethnographic studies of Alcoholics Anonymous (AA), show how the imitation of narrative practices serves to reinforce an initiate's identity as a recovering alcoholic and as a member of the AA community. As they discuss this community, the authors show how staying sober involves constructing a new identity, and storytelling is a major way this new identity is achieved. Telling the story of one's alcoholic life becomes a central feature of group membership. The stories told in AA have a particular structure and share particular themes. In the group self-conception, past events are supposed to be interpreted in certain ways, specific categories are to be used to classify past behavior, and certain conclusions are to be drawn from the story. The purpose of the storytelling is not to learn *from* the talk within the group, Lave and Wenger note, but is rather to learn *to* talk as a member of the group. Learning to talk and to tell a proper story in AA is not something that is overtly taught; rather, it is a skill that is learned through corrective trial-and-error and through imitation. As the imitation of storytelling practices becomes more advanced, the individual's understanding of her personal history begins to match that of others within the group. The imitative storytelling merges the individual's self-understanding, in other words, with the worldview of the larger community. Following an example, then, can change an individual's conceptions of the past so that it aligns with the understandings of the group.

Imitative Mediation of Present Conceptions of Group Membership

As Lave and Wenger point out, though, the imitative storytelling is not just oriented toward the past but also functions to designate group membership in the present. Through imitation, the novice provides markers in the present moment that designate the novice as part of a group. Through the activity of imitating members of a group, I affirm myself as a member of the community. The storytelling practices of AA not only function to mediate the past, for instance, but also serve as markers of community in the present. The same holds true for other social groups. Wearing a white lab coat or a mortarboard reinforces notions of being part of an academic group, and thus plays a role in the maintenance of community boundaries. Further, as Isocrates appears to indicate, the meaning of imitation in the present is infused both with what is observed and with what is unobserved. When I imitate a model by doing a specific action, it is a sign that I am part of a common set of people who do this specific action. And, as the model and I continue our common actions, we simultaneously suggest the formation of a more general set of people who do the same sort of things. Indeed, sometimes the imitation of only one action—an action to which the group attaches great importance—implies the acceptance of other aspects of the group's norms and standards. It suggests the adoption of a larger community teleology. In this sense, the meaning of imitation expands beyond the present action and reaches into the future.

Imitative Mediation of Future Conceptions of Group Membership

The repetition of action creates the possibility of a collective approach to the future. It does so in two different senses. The first sense in which imitation promotes cooperative future action is that imitation creates a common field of discourse to utilize when engaging shared problems. Because our repertoire of actions is similar within an imitative group, and because our interpretive activities are also similar, it is easier for us to cooperate on common tasks and questions. Adoption of similar interpretative strategies within a group allows group members to tackle questions of, say, textual interpretation with a common vocabulary and set of assumptions. This facilitates a cooperative effort that reaches into the future. It lays out a future program of cooperative work by, among other things, allowing us to talk to one another.

The second sense in which imitative action promotes cooperative action has to do with how imitation promotes common areas of concern. The actions we perform and the methods we use to solve problems influence the topics and questions we find productive and interesting. Indeed, topics of interest may themselves be the subject of imitation. After all, a new member of a group may become interested in a problem because she is imitating the interests and attitudes of those around her. So imitation, then, not only provides a set of common tools necessary for a cooperative effort in the face of problems, but it also seems to mediate the sorts of problems that are deemed important in the first place. The imitation of actions, methods, and interests creates conditions conducive to future collective action.

It appears, then, that imitation temporally mediates group membership by reshaping a new initiate's view of the past, present, and future. It is important to note that the imitated practices themselves may appear inconsequential to the larger, stated purposes of the group. White lab coats seem to have little to do with the practice of science; the uniforms could just as well be blue T-shirts or pink pullovers. In fact, there need not be any common dress at all. While the particular practice of wearing white lab coats has little to do (intrinsically) with science, the trivial practice may matter a great deal in staking out and maintaining group membership. This is a point that has important educational implications. The idea that imitative behavior helps to create communities of cooperative practice that transcend any intrinsic importance of the actions themselves is a powerful notion in forming educational community identity.[4]

Of course, it is also the case that imitation can drive groups apart. In *Violence and the Sacred* (1977), René Girard has gone so far as to argue that mimesis is essentially conflictual. By bringing one person's desire in line with another's, imitation leads to rivalry, competition, and conflict. Children often imitate one another in the toys they play with. This creates conditions in which toys become scarce, and the scarcity then creates conditions of conflict among the children. In playing with a toy, a particular child might become both a model for other children, and at the same time, become an obstacle to those children once they begin to imitate.[5] Imitation creates a group of children who play with the same toys, and this leads to fights, tears, and consternation. Sometimes, then, the same forces that bring the group together can eventually undermine the group. While imitation often mediates groups constructively, it can also work destructively. In either case, the power of imitation to mediate group membership should not be underestimated.

IMITATION, INITIATION, AND EDUCATION

The temporal mediation of community identity has much to do with the idea of *initiation*—the process by which an individual becomes part of a social group. If we make the connection between imitative meanings and initiation, educational implications begin to surface. Some philosophers of education, among them R. S. Peters (1965), have argued that education is essentially a process of initiation.

Education is the process by which we begin to enter cultural discussions, activities, and groups. If initiation is central to education, and if imitation is linked to initiation, then imitation must play a central role in educational communities.

Imitation can be involved in the process of initiation on several levels. Initiation may involve a singular imitative action, which serves as a right of passage. Within a specifically bounded context, the new member imitates the past actions of those who have gone before—they may go out alone into the wilderness, or eat unpalatable substances, or participate in a ceremonial dance, just as other members of the group have done before them. Those who imitate the rite of passage are considered part of the group. Initiation may also involve, however, not simply a one-time imitation, but also extended imitation over time. It might involve repeatedly replicating the actions of a leader, and this imitation might serve as continuing initiation into the group. Finally, imitation might also relate to initiation through a process of imitative learning. By observing a master, a new member may acquire the skills necessary to do the work of the group. An apprentice may watch a master, and through observation eventually be able to develop her own masterpiece—a marker that shows she has the skills to be considered part of a group. Under this model of initiation, it is not the imitation itself that serves as the initiation; rather, imitation promotes the development of the skills necessary to be initiated. The skills, learned through imitation, are the markers of group identity. There are several different ways, then, that imitation may be linked to initiation in general. Educational communities would not be exempt: Educational communities, like other communities, utilize imitative meanings to create a sense of we-ness that spans past, present, and future.

There is much to say about how the social meanings of imitation influence classroom communities. Within educational communities, for instance, imitative actions do not need to have any intrinsically deep significance. Common participation in educational rituals, even though they have little to do with the subject matter, may create a broader community of people who "do the same thing." This development of community through imitation can focus on the past by helping students sculpt joint narratives about the experiences they have had together as a class. It may involve constructing a joint narrative about a field trip, for example, which begins a process of reflection on their common experiences and developing, in a sense, a common (and imitative) historical hermeneutic. In this way, imitation can be used to shape past notions of community identity. Imitation in the present can be fostered by the use of common markers of classroom identity. Athletic teams are, again, examples of groups that often use uniforms and common rituals to mark group identity in the present. Imitative participation in a common historical hermeneutic and in common activities in the present necessarily points toward the future. Class members can be urged to collectively find and imitate past examples of successful problem solving, and thus be given a shared field of discourse for future inquiry.

Once we recognize the role of imitation in educational initiation, however, many problems and questions immediately arise. The first problem is how we are to recognize imitation within educational communities. How do we distinguish between imitation and, say, collective conformity to an exteriorly imposed norm? Usually, common actions come about through both types of processes. In fact, any one member of the community may have a difficult time specifying why she is doing what she is doing—is she following a rule that others are also following or is she imitating what others are doing? Even though it is often difficult to isolate the reason for acting within communities, these differences matter. It seems to me, for example, that we experience communities built around imitation often to be richer than groups whose collective action is based on conformity to rules. There is a difference between students creating communities themselves by wearing similar T-shirts and students wearing uniforms because a school told them to do so. The first sort of group has a clearer bond among students than does the second group. The imitative group is motivated by an internal sense of communality; the second group is motivated by a power from outside. For this reason, the teacher's job is not so much to enforce identical actions; rather, the job is to create the conditions conducive to collective imitation. The teacher can wear a lab coat during a science experiment, make lab coats available for the students to use, and arrange the social context so that imitative meanings cast the lab coat wearing in a positive light. If students resist such promptings, then the rebellious actions themselves may become subsequent markers of community, markers that would have both difficult and promising educational potential.

A serious problem with linking community construction to imitative actions, however, is that such a community may end up being exclusive, tribalistic, and intellectually rigid. It will necessarily drive the nonconformist (the nonimitator) from the community. Of course, any sort of community will have issues with conformity versus nonconformity; communities that are constructed around imitation are often no worse than other sorts of communities (for example, no worse than those that create conformity through obedience to exteriorly imposed rules). Exclusion is a problem for any idea of classroom community.

Now, if we recognize the role of imitation in communities, it seems that there are at least two possible responses to the problem of rigid exclusion in educational communities. The first option is to throw out the idea that classrooms should be communities (since communities will always be exclusive, in some sense) and use what we know about the power of imitative meaning to discourage the formation of communities. We would thus create contexts that work against imitation. The second option is to find a way in which imitation can be used to foster more flexible, open communities. To me, this second option seems preferable because of the benefits that come with the idea of communities (feelings of trust that allow for intellectual risk taking, concern for others, and so forth). Rather than throwing out the idea that classrooms should be communities, it seems we should instead ask whether some sorts of imitation can foster openness, creativity, and inclusion rather than closing off novelty and difference. The question of how imitation can foster openness is crucial, and it will be taken up with some depth in the chapters that follow.

A final question surrounding imitative social groups has to do with the possible conflict between the classroom ideals of community and the abhorrence of things like plagiarism. If students begin to imitate one another, they will likely become a community, no doubt, but they may also display behavior that sometimes looks like cheating. Plagiarism is a worry both because of its tendency to close down individual learning and inquiry and also because of its moral dimensions. It is immoral, it is often said, to replicate the ideas and work of another and to pass them off as one's own. The problem with condemning imitative communities on these grounds, however, is that not all work that replicates what another has done is viewed as a moral affront. That is to say, imitation does not always mean cheating. It is not simply an attempt to escape work; it can also be part of an initiation into a sphere of work. What factors, then, contribute to the meanings that are produced in an imitative moment? Why is one instance of imitation classified as cheating while another is taken as an invitation to cooperate? Why are imitative actions classified so differently?

FACTORS INFLUENCING IMITATIVE MEANING

I have described a significant array of possible meanings that are attached to the imitation of others. There are meanings relating to the individuals involved—to the model, the imitator, and third-party observers—and to the imitated actions themselves. Imitation can communicate a positive message or a negative message; it can communicate worship and esteem or ridicule and disdain. It can open up a moment of contemplation by serving as a mirror of self-examination or by acting as a gauge to test one's development of virtue. Of particular interest to educators is the idea that imitation can serve to temporally mediate community membership. Imitation marks out the groups we belong to and serves as a powerful instrument of reinterpreting past, present, and future. Given this range of possible meanings, it is helpful to examine the principles that govern the emergence of imitative meaning. Is there a sort of grammar that can help us comprehend the different messages and meanings presented by imitation?

Any attempt to find a universal grammar of imitation is probably impossible, just as it would be with other forms of language. There exists a tangled web of conditions and subconditions that will influence the meaning an imitation is taken to have. From what can be gathered from the literature and from what seems to be the case when certain scenarios are imagined, however, imitative meaning seems to partially depend on a number of key factors. These are some of the factors that appear to matter as we extract meaning from imitation:

1. *The relative status of the model and imitator.* If a person of high status within a particular action-framework is imitating somebody else, it often means something different to all relevant parties than if someone of low status is imitating.[6] Imitation by a person of high status, for example, may have a greater positive meaning to the model than imitation by a person with low status. We often want to be identified through imitation with the high-status person, but not the low-status person.

2. *The status and purpose of the action.* When imitation involves an action or achievement that has intrinsic worth, it will have a different meaning than when an action or achievement is merely instrumental to another goal.[7] If someone copies the way a piano is played (which may be an end in itself), for instance, it means something different than copying how oil is changed (which is instrumental to a larger goal). If people suspect that an imitation is merely an act of social influence, they also respond differently. For example, if people suspect that I am imitating someone in order to ingratiate myself with her, they are likely to perceive my actions negatively (see Jones, Jones, & Gergen, 1963).

3. *The confidence of the model and imitator.* Imitative action has a different meaning depending on whether someone has high confidence in what they are doing or has low confidence in what they
are doing. A low-confidence model, for example, might take great
comfort in seeing others doing what she is doing, as this would
serve as an acknowledgment of her competence.

4. *The constraint (or facilitation) that the imitation presents for future
action.* If relevant parties are impeded in future action by the
imitation, then the imitation is likely to have a different meaning than when future action is not impeded. For example, if
people imitate a master fisherman by always using his favorite
spots, the fisherman is more likely to react negatively to the
imitation because it limits his future fishing possibilities (these
are precisely the considerations that led Girard to say that imitation necessarily breeds conflict). If the model stands to profit
by being the only one associated with an action, obviously, then
imitation will also be taken in the negative way.

5. *The context of signs surrounding the imitation.* The language, facial
expressions, and bodily posture of the imitator matter a great
deal to the interpretation of imitation. These sorts of things
often trump all other factors. A person with low confidence
could be imitated by a high-status imitator and we would nor-
mally expect the model to take a positive meaning from the
imitation. But if the imitator imitates with a sarcastic laugh and
a sneer, then that trumps the other considerations. The imitation will be taken negatively, as an act of mockery or derision.

6. *The ideological context that surrounds the imitation.* The meaning
of imitation also depends on certain cultural beliefs concerning individualism, respect, worship, replication of actions,
and so forth. If there is a belief that all actions should be of
one's own creation and initiation, imitation will be taken
more negatively.

These factors, and certainly many others, combine in particular
contexts to create the meaning of the imitation. One of the most important ways these combine is to construct the idea of ownership over
a particular action or achievement. Some actions we perform we feel
we own, others we do not. Further, we want to be *identified* with the
actions and achievements we feel belong to us. The ownership of an
action has to do with the "status and nature of the action" (factor 2

above), but it also involves some of the other factors. What counts as something we own derives from the ideologies of individualism and ownership within our given cultural context. Who is entitled to claim ownership is a function of the social milieu.

In Western culture, a common assumption is that we own the products of our labor. This notion of ownership is most fully articulated in John Locke's *Second Treatise on Government*, in which Locke argues that mixing work with natural resources connects the individual to the resulting product. The person who contributes labor to the resource has a right to the final product, a right that "excludes it from the common right of other men." For Locke, an apple becomes a man's, not when he boils it, eats it, or digests it. "[I]t is plain," he writes, "if the first gathering made them not his, nothing else could. That labour put a distinction between them and common" (1690/1997, §27). Whatever the problems are with this view as a way of justifying ownership (and there are many), Locke has done an admirable job of capturing commonsense intuitions of ownership, both in his time and ours. Something becomes ours, we tend to feel, when we have invested our time, talents, and resources into transforming it into what it is.

The idea of ownership plays a large part in the meanings we assign to imitative action. Consider a tourist who is trying to learn how to pay a bus fare in an unfamiliar city. Suppose that, in order to find out what to do, the tourist watches several local people use the electronic device that is used to pay the fare and then imitates what they do to purchase the ticket. Finally, suppose that one of the locals sees the tourist imitating her actions. What is her reaction likely to be? We would find it odd for her to care about this copying behavior, even though the tourist directly copied and exploited her knowledge of the bus system without any acknowledgment. The model is unlikely to make the charge of "plagiarism." Why? The procedure of paying the bus fare is probably not an action she claims to have invented in any way. The local has not invested time, talents, or resources into the procedure and thus probably does not care to be identified or known by that activity. In addition, outside observers would not find the imitation very meaningful even if they noticed the imitation. This particular imitative act may serve to acknowledge the local as an expert user of the city's public transportation system and the imitator as someone dependent and needy, perhaps, but it is taken to say very little else about the model or the imitator—at least from an ethical point of view.

Now compare this situation to an artist who develops a painting technique. Information on this painting technique may be valuable, just like the information proved valuable to the tourist in the unfamiliar city. If the artist were to be watched closely and imitated, however, the artist would likely care a great deal about the imitation. Perhaps the artist would be honored by the imitation and would enjoy the recognition that might come from helping others to develop a new technique. Or, perhaps more likely, the artist would accuse the imitator of plagiarism. The imitation of an action, or of a product of an action, that is intrinsically valuable to the model will often provoke a protective response. Whatever the exact reaction would be, though, it does seem that, in situations like these, people *care* that they are being copied (unlike the situation with the bus fare). A painting technique is more likely to bring with it royalties and a sense of ownership, and hence, be more closely tied to an individual's sense of identification. Ownership of the action makes the imitation more salient. It often is what turns an imitation into a plagiarism.

The specifics of how one appropriates the work of others have long played an essential part in the valuation of imitative action. D. A. Russell (1979) points out that Latin literature, although it was filled with imitative writing, still exhibited a concern for literary theft or plagiarism. What separated a successful imitator from a plagiarist were two points. First, the imitator must acknowledge the model. This acknowledgment does not come about through the use of footnotes; rather, it comes about as the "tenor" of one's writing reveals an awareness of tradition. Second, the imitator must make a piece of writing his or her own through selection, modification, and bold deviation from the model at key junctures. When Latin writers put their own stamp of ownership over largely replicated passages, they avoided the ancient equivalent to the charge of plagiarism. The sense of proper individual ownership is what altered the meaning of the imitation. The poet individualized the work of another, while at the same time appropriating it. This individualization allowed the writer to achieve a personal identification with the copied material.

Identity is not something we attach only to individuals, but also to groups. After all, a group can have its own sense of identification. Accordingly, the idea of ownership operates not only on the level of individual identity, but also on the level of group identity. Indeed, an essential feature of understanding the meanings that attach to imitation involves the idea of *group* ownership. Groups come to feel that they have ownership of certain actions, styles, products, and ways of life, just as individuals do. Groups can and do imitate other groups. Imitation is often viewed favorably when done by individuals within a group (intragroup imitation), but may be viewed very unfavorably when attempted by those on the outside (intergroup imitation). In cases such as these, it is the group that has claimed ownership of the action, and this means that the action has come to be a marker of group identity. The factors that change imitative meaning among individuals also function to change the meaning among groups.

A sense of group ownership is what gives imitative action its central meanings with regard to communities of practice. If members of the group do not collectively own an action, then intragroup imitation of the action is likely to be viewed as a form of cheating or plagiarism. It will be viewed as a moral offense. If the group, however, is thought to own the action or product, rather than the individual, the meaning will be different. Since the action is "ours," not "mine" or "yours," repeating the action can become a way of affirming group membership rather than cheating.

IMITATION AND COMMUNITIES OF LEARNING

Education is, in many ways, about fostering particular sorts of communities. The idea of community is important in educational settings in at least two different ways. First, it is often said that we want members of a particular class or school to themselves be a community of learning. The community within the school allows for more meaningful educational interactions. Second, we also want learners to feel that they are members of larger communities of human practice— members of larger democratic, scholarly, literate, and scientific communities. Imitation plays a role in mediating both forms of community membership. The power of imitation in education resides not only in learning through imitating action, it appears, but in learning in and through the communities that imitation helps to construct and regulate. One key in constructing communities is to foster an educationally sensitive idea of collective ownership. That is to say, imitative actions that have meaning conducive to the formation of educational communities (rather than meanings involving mockery and plagiarism) often involve the collective ownership of an action. How can this sense of community ownership of action be fostered?

One significant clue to forming educational communities relates to Locke's psychological insight about when we feel justified in "owning" something. We feel justified in owning something, he says, when we have produced the product by means of our own labor. If this is true (and it seems to be at least partially true as a descriptive claim), then a sense of group ownership comes about when a group invests its labor in producing a joint product. This product may be a certain type of achievement (and end result) or way of doing things (a method). To give classroom groups a feeling of community, the product must then allow for subsequent contributions and extended development through the involvement of class members. As class members participate in the development of the product through imitation, a sense of common ownership will be created and hence a feeling of community. If the ownership is seen as a collective thing, it is less likely to possess the meanings that lead to charges of plagiarism.

For other students to participate in the product or practice, it is essential that it be openended and expandable. Rather than imitating particular things that are made or conclusions that are reached, it would be better for the imitation to focus on particular processes of creation.[8] Imitation, for instance, could involve the idea of imitation in experimentation. If one student has had a great success conducting an experiment or building a scientific device, teachers could build on such success by facilitating subsequent imitation revolving around practices of experimentation or building research tools. In cases like these, classroom imitation could be rather abstract, but as I have already emphasized, often seemingly trivial imitative actions may supplement and support the larger activities of the group. The class may not only build their own scientific instruments, but they may also wear similar lab coats or T-shirts that say "The Knowledge Builders" or some other more meaningful phrase. In this way, the abstract imitation of the collectively owned product (imitating processes of research) would be made concrete by visible markers of group identity. Once the community is flourishing through cooperative imitation, all the educational benefits that flow from such communities would then follow.

An emphasis on openended imitation of process also provides clues to solving the problems of imitation that Girard brings up. Imitation often means that multiple people are pursuing the same objects. This creates scarcity, for Girard, and scarcity produces rivalry and conflict. For this reason, the object of imitation must be something that does not operate within a framework of scarcity. There must be enough of what is imitated to go around. The focus on imitation must allow for multiple students to participate in the activity without taking away the possibility for others to participate on an equal basis. Otherwise, imitation will eventually tear down the community instead of building it up.

Locke's idea of labor producing a sense of ownership over products and actions can also be used in making connections to larger communities outside the classroom. At first, making connections to these outside groups may seem difficult. After all, it may be difficult to help the class achieve a sense of ownership of and identification with the practices of seemingly distant scientific and scholarly communities. There are ways, though, to help students to participate in the real labor of such groups (to imitate the practices of the group in productive ways), and to thereby create a sense of community. Some projects, like the GLOBE Program,[9] in which students—in imitation of scientists—compile real environmental data and present the data in an online repository, demonstrate that students can make real contributions to the outside communities. In such programs, students begin to feel a part of larger communities of inquiry; they come to a sense of ownership of outside activities. The feeling of community comes not only from an initial cooperative project, but also from continual participation in that product through imitation (the "product" in this case being scientific practice). More trivial markers (wearing lab coats or producing video scientific documentaries) will also help them feel like part of a larger community. So group ownership, and continued collective imitation, creates communities both within and without the classroom walls.

One temptation when building a community will be for the community to form around imitation of the teacher. Although classroom communities may often involve imitation of the teacher, critical meanings can also be conveyed when the teacher is the one who imitates. Imitation of the student is one way teachers can show interest and attention to the student. A teacher's high-status position and a beginning student's lack of confidence will often result in the teacher's imitation being well received and taken by the student as a sign of teacher confidence. Perhaps most important, a teacher's imitation of the students will often be a powerful way to affirm the sense of community. The teacher says by imitation, "I respect you," "I support you," and, "I am a part of the group rather than its master and overseer." Similarly, the students can send such messages to each other through imitation, if the right balance of factors can be found. The meanings involved with imitation can play a central role in effective classroom communication.

CONCLUSION

Imitation is not the only factor that builds a social group, but it is an important avenue in creating and refining our communities. Marcel Kinsbourne (2005) has written about how "imitation is more about affiliation and attachment than about learning, although it may be about learning too" (p. 167). Through imitation, our actions become rhythmically synchronized with one another; that is, we become "entrained." We synchronize not only our actions but our attitudes and thinking. "Rhythmic social entrainment," he writes, "is more intimately compelling than reasoned argument in inducing two, to many, to adopt the same point of view" (p. 172).

This statement is true, but also troubling. I have argued that imitation can play an important and positive role in the formation of educational communities. Clearly, there is also a dark side to imitation in communities. As I have already suggested, if classroom communities are built on imitation, there seems to be little room for creativity, criticality, novelty, or difference in any form. Imitation can impede what is of most value in education, the creation of skills of open deliberation and inquiry. This seems to be particularly problematic when we talk about moral education, an endeavor that, it has often been argued, cannot ultimately be based on imitation.

There are, however, certain classes of entrainment and imitation that are useful in deliberation, including moral deliberation. In other words, there are certain types of imitation that are useful in reasoning and learning. With these types of imitation, the imitative community may exist for the sake of learning, and the rhythmic entrainment may entrain so as to promote critical thought. One of the key questions for educators relates to how the entrainment can be harnessed so as to promote deliberation rather than impede it. A discussion of the problem of imitation, deliberation, and moral education will be the focus of the next chapter.

CHAPTER 6

Imitation, Exemplarity, and Moral Reason

The historical tradition has made various assumptions about the relationship between imitation and human reason. Some have argued that imitation is, or can be, a crowning achievement of successful practical reason. Imitation of good models, especially for the Classical tradition, is an expression of human wisdom. Imitation has been thought to be somehow compatible with autonomous thought and expression. Others, particularly those under the influence of Enlightenment epistemic individualism, have thought otherwise. Imitative action is offering a counterfeit self; it is a forgetfulness or a type of suicide. By this, the authors have meant that imitating others, or doing something because others do it, is a negation of our individual capacity to reason and it is directly opposed to autonomous and creative action. This uneasy relationship between reason and imitation has already appeared in the previous chapter as we examined the relationship between imitative action and educational communities.

Two important arguments against focusing on the imitation of examples in moral education are what I will call the "practical objection" and the "theoretical objection." According to the practical objection, if human examples are playing a comprehensive role in moral reasoning, then such reasoning will produce bad practical consequences, at least under certain contextual conditions. In a context that demands flexibility, for instance, one cannot simply do what an example once did. The theoretical objection, in contrast, finds a logical incompatibility between following examples and praiseworthy moral reasoning.

According to the theoretical objection, following an example involves doing an action simply because "someone else is doing it" and this can never be an adequate moral reason for action. Morally praiseworthy reasons involve doing something because it is the right thing to do or because one is concerned with the welfare of somebody else. The practical and the theoretical objections are intended to show that examples are, in the end, of limited value in moral reasoning and moral education. Examples of human life cannot play a comprehensive role in moral education.

In the preceding chapters, I have proposed a way of thinking about human examples in education that attends closely to the intricacies of social context. Along the way, I have suggested that this way of thinking about examples will be useful in educational theory and practice. These problems of imitation and moral reasoning are such cases. Indeed, a greater social understanding of exemplarity helps to answer these objections to a comprehensive role for human examples. Learning to follow an explicit example is certainly not the only important way of learning about ethics, of course, but a social understanding of imitation can show us that examples do more productive work than has previously been thought in the Enlightenment tradition. In arguing for a positive role for examples in education, I will explore the assumptions that have been made about imitation and reason. This analysis will serve to counter the critics who argue that focusing on human examples is necessarily unreasonable, unwise, and otherwise contrary to a proper understanding of ethical judgment.

THE PRACTICAL OBJECTION TO IMITATING EXAMPLES

The practical objection to imitation in moral education is this: Following examples of past conduct will often lead to bad practical decisions. To represent this position, I will use the work of Edmund Erde, a medical ethicist who discusses the use of role models in the moral education of physicians. In order to do justice to the depth of his objections, it will be necessary to explain the arguments in some detail. First, Erde admits that it is sometimes impossible to specify in language every aspect of a social role and that "relying on role models is desirable, perhaps even necessary, for some level of role specification" (Erde, 1997, p. 34). At the same time, though, Erde argues, "Conceptual and ethical dangers haunt our relying on role models" (p. 37). He strongly objects to the virtue theory emphasis on role models and argues for what he calls a Socratic education. For Erde, the essence of ethics is "philosophizing," or the development of "careful, reasoned positions that withstand scrutiny." It involves "the ability to innovate and exercise independent moral judgment" (p. 38). "One might hope," he continues, "that students could do this on their own—or at least that strong, courageous, and self-aware students could resist dependent copying" (p. 38).

Erde's first major reason for thinking that role models are insufficient is that roles are constantly changing and contested in a pluralistic, dynamic society. To understand Erde's concern, one need only think of technological change and how it alters the role of medical doctors. Under current conditions, a physician who is found using the same tools and techniques as a long deceased mentor would come under suspicion. After all, the state-of-the-art would have certainly changed since then. Continuous technological change means that the physician needs to be able to evaluate new developments in an independent way (that is, independent from the practices of early models). An imitation-based education seems to lock the learner into one way of acting, while technological change demands that we constantly adapt to new standards and situations. More flexible types of action are needed than what imitative action (and imitative learning) can provide. Imitation thus appears to be inherently and damagingly conservative.

Social expectations surrounding roles can also change, sometimes drastically. In many ways, being a doctor means something different today than it did even twenty years ago. People have different expectations about how a doctor should behave. The possibility of social change demands that students be flexible about the normative dimensions of their profession. A doctor who treats her patients exactly as her mentor did will be ill equipped to adapt to changing social expectations. The physician needs to be able to evaluate the demands of her role from an independent viewpoint. Further, roles are always contested. Simply following the example of a mentor is insufficient because it assumes that the mentor properly fulfilled the role of a physician. Since the role of physician is highly contested territory in a pluralistic society, one should never assume that the actions of a model are appropriate across contexts. Students thus need to be able to judge for themselves what the role of a doctor actually requires, apart from what they have seen their mentors doing. An education that emphasizes the imitation of role models may impart an unrealistic dogma to students that will hamper them in their future roles. We want students to be able to question their roles in an open and independent way.

Another line of argument suggests that people deserve to hear justifiable reasons for actions that affect them. Students will need to be able to explain and defend their decisions to others (such as patients, colleagues, staff, and so forth). Offering good reasons for one's actions, and listening to the reasons offered by others, is one way we show respect for other human beings. Imitation, however, does not necessarily involve the development of the ability to give or receive reasons. Doing something because somebody else does it is not a reason that other people will or should accept. So an education based on role models does not help students develop ethically sensitive discursive skills.

Finally, the fact the one can learn a role by imitating a model already assumes that the learner has a theory about what features of the model are relevant to imitate. Exemplarity is always theory dependent. Erde writes, "Without an account of a behavior there are too many variable interpretations of it available, and no one could automatically tell which features of the case motivate or direct the model. In other words, the student is not in a position to know when she has the same (type of) case or is doing the same thing as the model did" (1997, p. 37).[1] Thus, it is misguided to emphasize exemplars over ethical theory because a theory is necessary to learn anything from exemplars. An "account of a behavior" must always come first. We had thus better be sure that we are able to defend our moral theories apart from the examples we learned from as we were educated.

In sum, Erde contends that focusing too much on role models may bring bad consequences, especially in a rapidly changing, pluralistic world of contested social roles and values. Such circumstances require that students think creatively and autonomously, going beyond what has been done before to find independent reasons for who they are and what they do. Critics would also argue that focusing too much on models is incoherent, since models are meaningless without some theory to tell the learner what to pay attention to. Although Erde thinks that role models certainly have a place in moral education, he cautions that overstating the importance of models is a mistake. Moral reasoning needs to be more flexible, creative, and critical than examples alone can promote.

To the extent that critics like Erde argue against an overreliance on human exemplars in teaching, their point is surely correct: Multiple methods of teaching always seem better than strict reliance on any singular method. Having agreed on this, however, the question becomes how much emphasis constitutes an overemphasis. I believe that good arguments can be marshaled to show that many of the practical concerns advanced by the critics of imitation, like Erde, fail to realize how far following examples can actually go in meeting their concerns. One key to seeing how far exemplarity can go is, again, to place human exemplarity in its proper social context. An understanding of exemplarity in its social context should encourage us to blur the distinction between imitative action on the one hand, and critical, flexible, and creative action on the other.

A SOCIAL RESPONSE TO THE PRACTICAL OBJECTION

Imitation and Creative Communities

The first way to blur the distinctions among criticality, flexibility, creativity, and imitation is to understand that imitation serves to temporally mediate and regulate communities of inquiry. This point was argued in detail in the previous chapter. Imitation of storytelling procedures allows people to see the events of their past lives as uniting under similar interpretative patterns; it provides markers in the present that designate the novice as part of a community; and, through the imitation of actions, methods, and interests, it creates conditions conducive to future collective action. Imitation supplies the tools and attitudes for a future-oriented concern for common problems. This community-regulation feature of exemplars is not by itself good or bad; it simply describes what happens as communities form and develop.

If imitation plays a role in the temporal maintenance of communities, then it will also influence communities of inquiry and creativity. The scientific community, for instance, is based on imitation at many levels—from styles of dress, to methods of communication and investigation, to future problems of interest. Yet, few would deny that the scientific community is a good example of a community of inquiry. Critics who say that imitative behavior is damagingly conservative tend to ignore the role of such behavior in bringing together communities that cooperatively work on shared problems. Although any particular imitative action may seem uncreative, inflexible, and uncritical, when the action is taken in its larger social context, it can often be shown to play a role in forming and maintaining these communities. And these communities, in turn, may be acting in ways that are very creative, flexible, and critical. Indeed, these communities of inquiry may be essential to navigating problems of social change, role contestation, and so forth.

What alerted me to this idea was reflecting on the group of friends I spent time with as an adolescent. There was a lot of behavioral matching, including a good deal of imitative behavior, within this group. The imitative actions probably looked quite thoughtless at times.

Indeed, my parents sometimes worried about the perceived thought-lessness of such imitations by asking questions like, "If your friends jumped off a cliff, would you?" The imitative behavior formed us into a community, though, and in this community we felt free to discuss important questions late into the night—such conversations were prob-ably my first taste of philosophy, although I didn't recognize it at the time. This community, based in part on imitative action, also pro-moted inquiry. An even better example would be to think of a school of artists, like the Impressionists, where a great deal of imitation took place within the school, but the school went on to produce revolution-ary and groundbreaking artistic achievements.

This is not to say, of course, that all imitative communities pro-duce creative inquiry all of the time. In fact, some imitative commu-nities may impede inquiry as much as others promote it. Most communities probably promote inquiry in one sense while closing it down in another. My argument is only that imitative actions play a role in building communities of cooperative action and that these communities may sometimes be communities of creative inquiry. This is enough to show that a creative, flexible, and critical inquiry is not *necessarily* in opposition to the imitation of examples. It is the commu-nity that is being creative, flexible, and critical, however, and not sim-ply the individual.

Of course, the imitation of examples, by itself, is not what pro-duces the creative or critical actions. It simply helps to form the com-munity—the sense of we-ness—that makes collective action possible. For collective action to turn into collective inquiry or creativity, some-thing more is required. The community and the collective action within communities must be of certain kind. A central educational question, then, would ask, What is this *something more* that is required for in-quiry within imitative communities? It seems to me that a partial answer to this question involves the factors that influence the mean-ings of imitation developed in the previous chapter. Creative commu-nities must feel a sense of collective ownership over an endeavor, and that endeavor must be openended and allow for subsequent develop-ment. The "product" of imitation in such cases often turns out to be a "process" with which the group collectively identifies.

Process Imitation versus Results Imitation

A significant distinction to make when discussing imitative learning has to do with the difference between "result imitation" and "process imitation." Employing this distinction is another way to blur the dis-

action

tinctions between criticality, flexibility, and creativity, on the one hand, and imitative action, on the other. It suggests that some imitation can produce novel results. The distinction also helps us understand why some imitative social communities become communities of inquiry.

Result imitation is the reproduction of the results that come at the end of a particular creative process. Think of a composer who imitates the musical forms developed by another composer, or think of a businessperson who reproduces the sales decisions made by a more experienced colleague. In contrast, process imitation involves the reproduction of a process that produces the results. Think of a physician who imitates a mentor's decision-making process by always listening to the concerns of patients, seeking the advice of other healthcare professionals, and taking time to think things over. This process imitation is very different from the result-oriented type of imitation.

In the case of imitating the results of an action, it does indeed seem that the products of such imitation will be inflexible, uncritical, and uncreative, and probably ill-suited to meeting the problems of a pluralistic and dynamic environment. This is the sort of thing the critics of imitation should certainly be worried about. The imitation of processes, though, offers the possibility of the creation of novelty. Imitating a process of creation may produce widely varying results.[2] A composer may imitate her mentor by walking through the woods while composing, and this creative process may lead to new creative achievements. Similarly, someone may imitate a particular deliberative process (as in the case of the physician) and may end with unique and unprecedented decisions. Imitating such actions as "taking time to think and talk things over" may facilitate an openended inquiry. It is possible to imitate a Socrates.

Imitative action, then, when it reproduces certain creative processes, can produce results that are highly original, creative, and independently justifiable. Indeed, sometimes groups acting in this way can be more original, creative, and critical than any one individual working alone. The Enlightenment tradition and its suspicions of imitation are based on overly individualistic interpretations of reason and creativity. Many, if not all, of the most prominent achievements of human creativity and reason (again, think of artistic traditions) involve some degree of imitation.

One might object to this response and claim that, even in process imitation, the imitator is still too bound by what has gone before. After all, this process imitation would preclude the introduction of new processes of inquiry and creation. It would prevent any needed revolution in methods and approaches and would thus be poorly suited to a dynamic, pluralistic society. In response, it need only be said that a sort of revolutionary exemplarity regarding processes is also a real possibility. With a revolutionary example of human life, I imitate not a product or even a process of doing things; rather, I imitate rule breaking. In this case, I imitate a rule breaker by breaking the rules of the existing creative processes. The action that is replicated (rule breaking) is abstract, to be sure, but still a viable type of imitation. Someone could still object, I suppose, that this imitative rule breaker is not really breaking all the rules because one rule is still sacred—namely, the rule to break the rules—and a metalevel conservatism is thus still intact. Even this sort of imitation is still working within the framework of the model—the exemplar itself is not criticized. But by this point, however, the problems posed by the practical objection are far distant, since imitation has been shown to be able to sometimes produce rule-breaking actions—something that might indeed be necessary in a dynamic society. There would be no *pragmatic* difference between someone who is herself a creative rule breaker and someone who imitates, in an abstract way, the activity of creative rule breaking. The metalevel conservatism does not matter when answering the practical objection.

Imitation and Novelty

While critics of imitation may underestimate the presence of imitation in high-level human practices, they may overestimate the extent to which the imitation is slavish and lacking in novelty. An imitated action is *never* an exact replication of an action; it is always different, if only in the time and space in which the action is performed. I never do the exact thing as somebody else. I always do it in different circumstances, with a different accent, and with a different personal history. All imitation, one could say, is thus "creative" and "novel" in some sense. What people like Erde desire is the ability to produce novel and flexible responses to a dynamic and pluralistic situation. But they do not just want sheer novelty in action: *Any* imitation produces novelty in some sense. Instead, what they want (rightly) is novelty with some sort of value attached to it, novelty that will contribute something. There is a difference, it seems, between a composer who copies Beethoven's symphonic form line for line and one who gives a valuable interpretation of Beethoven's symphonic form. Both imitate Beethoven, in some sense, and take Beethoven as an exemplar. The "interpreter," however, is generally thought to imitate in a creative way. Interpreting is a creative achievement while copying is not.

So what turns a novel replication (which is produced with *any* imitation) into a creative achievement? The literature in aesthetics on this point is vast. It seems clear, though, that the social value of a creative achievement at least partially depends on its participation in a community and in a tradition in some way, as well as its distinction from that community and tradition. Something that turned out to be *completely* novel—different in every important way from what had gone before—would seem like an absurdity rather than an achievement and would accordingly possess little social value (imagine, for instance, how Jackson Pollock would have been received in the Renaissance). The value of novelty depends on how an imitative action participates in a tradition and responds to a certain history. Valuable novelty contributes something to an ongoing story.

Notice, though, how this leads us back to imitation and how imitation mediates community membership. The value of novelty depends on the groups, communities, and traditions we belong to, and these things are mediated, at least in part, by imitation. Creation and criticality *depend* on imitation within traditions and communities as much as they reject the traditions and communities. It would be a mistake to deemphasize the role of imitation in the tradition of continuous practices (like medicine). People need to participate in communities to produce valuable novelty, and participation in communities often occurs through imitation.

Latin literature, where imitation was often present, again gives us a sense of how novelty and imitation can coexist. D. A. Russell (1979) has written about how Latin writers were expected to demonstrate their deep familiarity with a literary tradition by imitating some of the key writers and forms. However, the proper attitude toward the tradition was competition with the tradition through imitative expression: "The imitator must think of himself as competing with his model, even if he knows he cannot win" (p. 16). The imitator repeats in some sense what has gone before, to be sure, but the emphasis is on placing the repetition in a context that gives new and greater meaning to the words being repeated. Through imitation, the Latin writer connects with tradition while trying at the same time to outdo or expand it. In this way, the Latin literary tradition reconciled imitation with creativity.

Community and Reason Making

A final way of blurring the distinction between imitation and criticality relates to how the reasons are constructed for justifying a given action. Critics are adamant that students should be able to find independently

scaffold?

justifiable reasons for action, but they ignore the role imitation plays in the creation of meaning. In other words, this view again ignores the "invitational role" that human examples play in social groups. As an example brings forth imitation, the learner is drawn, not only into a particular line of action, but also into particular practices. As the learner participates in a community, she grasps the nuances of meaning that come from engaging in the community's form of life. From these nuances of meaning one can construct reasons for action. What John McDermott said of pragmatic belief can equally be said of imitation: It is the "wedge into the tissue of experience, for the purpose of liberating dimensions otherwise closed to the agnostic standpoint" (McDermott, 1967, p. xxx). Critics correctly say that students should be able to give reasons for their actions and that picking out exemplars requires some theory, but they seem to ignore the role that exemplars play in the construction of reasons and theories. Examples and imitation come together to construct a way of seeing that gives theories meaning.

Exemplars and the Practical Objection: Conclusion

Suppose we assume that all these arguments fail and a strong distinction between imitation and a critical education is still tenable. Would this justify deemphasizing role models, as critics suppose? Even then, it would not seem that we are justified in deemphasizing human exemplars because this criticism fails to take into account the nonimitative side of human exemplarity (see, for instance, the types of nonimitative exemplars discussed in chapter 2). One might agree that reason and creativity cannot be imitated, but it seems that not all educational examples of human life involve imitation. Human examples do many things. They provoke inspiration to attain an ideal, elicit questioning, open up new ways of seeing the world, and so forth. So even if we assume that imitation is opposed to the sort of reasoning that a dynamic, pluralistic society demands, we do not have license to forget about the educational import of other human lives.

Against the practical objections, then, I have argued that exemplars can play a central part in a creative, critical, and flexible moral reasoning. The centrality of examples is to be found in their social function. To understand the value of exemplars one must recognize that human exemplars can play an "invitational role" mediating communities of inquiry, that they can model creative processes rather than already created results, and that they can provoke questions as well as provide answers. So the answer to the question of whether human exemplars can play a central role in a creative, flexible, and critical process of moral reasoning should be affirmative. At least some types of exemplars can indeed promote criticality and creativity. A central role for examples in education is not necessarily opposed to an education that promotes critical thinking and creativity. What this means for educators is that the question is not how much we should emphasize role models in education, but is, rather, what sort of role models are to be emphasized. If we are interested in creativity and criticality in a dynamic and pluralistic society (as I agree we must be) then the best sorts of exemplars are those that initiate learners into processes of creation and give them access to communities that themselves produce valued achievements and that make creativity and criticality possible.

THE THEORETICAL OBJECTION TO IMITATING EXAMPLES

The second objection takes aim at the moral praiseworthiness of following and imitating past examples of proper conduct. Critics of imitation argue that imitation is a betrayal, or at least a troubling underutilization, of the human capacity for reason. Praiseworthy expression of morality in human life demands not only that we perform morally correct actions, but also that we do these actions for morally appropriate reasons.

Kant is perhaps the most famous advocate of the view that a "good will" is essential for any morally praiseworthy action. He draws a distinction between proper actions that have moral worth and those that do not. For the proper action to have moral worth, it must be done by someone with a good will—someone who does the moral action, not in hopes of gaining reward or status, for example, but because it is the right thing to do. In his *Grounding for the Metaphysics of Morals,* Kant uses an example of a shopkeeper to illustrate his point (1785/1993, p. 10). Giving all customers a fair price is the proper moral action, Kant maintains, but if that moral action springs from the shopkeeper's desire to maintain his reputation for the purpose of making money, the action is without moral worth. To have moral worth, the shopkeeper must do the right action *because* it is the right thing to do.

Although Kant is perhaps the best example of this way of thinking about ethics, he is certainly not alone. And although what counts as a right reason may vary among moral philosophers, most would agree on one thing: Doing something simply because "someone else is doing it" does not count as a very good reason for human action. Actions should be judged on their own merits, and using another

person's behavior as a reason for acting takes attention away from the
merits of the actions themselves. The fact that another person does
something does not seem to justify an act if it is wrong nor does it
serve as a praiseworthy reason for doing the right thing. Simply doing
something because somebody else does it is herd behavior, as Nietzsche
would say. It is the abrogation of human reason.

A SOCIAL RESPONSE TO THE THEORETICAL OBJECTION

There are at least two major ways of countering the theoretical objection. First, one could undercut the critic's premise and argue that the
intentions or reasons for an action should not play a significant role in
judging the moral praiseworthiness of a proper action. Second, one
could argue that the reasons involved with imitative action are not
incompatible with doing things in a morally praiseworthy way.

The first strategy, which breaks the link between praiseworthiness and acting for the right reasons, would involve a detailed analysis of ethical theory—a task well beyond the scope of this book and
somewhat tangential to the topic of exemplarity. Briefly, though, I will
say that it is not entirely clear that morally praiseworthy action must
be based on praiseworthy intentions—a utilitarian theorist, after all,
would deny that an agent's reasons or intentions should play a role in
moral evaluation (at least directly). Utilitarianism has a long intellectual pedigree, and the existence of such a view suggests that the question of whether intentions should be a factor in moral evaluation is
still open. At this point, though, let us assume the more commonly
held position that intentions and reasons for action do matter in moral
evaluation. To most people, I believe, it would matter if a philanthro-
pist were donating money only to promote her business interests. Most
of us would evaluate the action differently if we knew this to be the
motive (although we would still probably accept the donation).

More relevant to the topic of human exemplarity is the second
response that seeks to reexamine the moral status of reasons involved
in following exemplars. Are there reasons for following an example
that are morally praiseworthy reasons? And what is the status of the
reason "because someone else is doing it"? Again, there are at least
two ways of responding to these questions. First, one could argue that
the reasons for following an example are sometimes not "because
someone else is doing it." Second, one could argue that the reason
"because someone else is doing it" is itself a morally praiseworthy

reason or at least that it is on the same level with other reasons for action. Each of these responses is worth considering.

The first response may counter the critic by pointing to the long historical tradition of discourse surrounding human exemplarity. In the historical tradition, few proponents of imitation have suggested that the imitation of an action should be based on the reason "because someone else is doing it." Indeed, I have described the standard model of educational exemplarity and pointed out that, under this model, the example is a source of information about how to achieve certain ends—how to be an effective king, a good father, a real philosopher, and so forth. Through a careful analysis of the results of the example's actions, the observer decides whether imitation is appropriate. The reason for imitation is not "because somebody else is doing it." Instead, the example has provided information about how to achieve a particular result and it is this information that provides the reason for imitative action. The example provides evidence of the results of certain lines of action. It seems that acting on this evidence is not an abrogation of reason and, therefore, that this sort of imitation defeats the first theoretical objection. The desire is to obtain a particular consequence and the example gives us information about how to achieve the consequence. The desire is not to do the same thing as another. If we desire to help our neighbor, and we observe somebody helping their neighbor in creative ways, imitating that person is still morally praiseworthy. The motivation is to help, and the example shows us an effective way of helping. The model simply showed us new ways of doing something we wanted to do anyway.

There are several problems, however, with this response. We may agree that it can be reasonable and praiseworthy to imitate a model that has demonstrated a successful way of reaching an already accepted end. It is not as clear, however, whether it is also praiseworthy to adopt (or, more precisely, emulate) the *ends* of action from other people. It seems that the end of the action gives us a standard by which to intelligently judge the means to that end—the better means are what help us to better accomplish our ends. But if the end is the object of judgment, it is not as clear what is to be used as the standard. Since moral action has as much to do with the ends of action as it does with the means, it may be a problem if ends cannot be intelligently adopted from human exemplars.[3] By imitating the ends and desires of others, we seem to forgo the possibility of rational deliberation. If I want to help my neighbor because everyone else seems to be doing it, it not only seems less morally praiseworthy than if it stemmed from my desires directly, it also becomes dangerous. After all, if everyone else were being cruel, then I would follow those examples too.

Furthermore, throughout the previous chapters I have tried to undermine the standard model as the ultimate description of exemplarity and education. The standard model, I have argued, does not exhaust all the ways in which human exemplars can influence human lives. I have argued that it is often the case that examples are not chosen *by* the learner, but are instead chosen *for* the learner by surrounding social contexts. I have also argued that imitation does not come about as the learner finds reasons and motivation to imitate a model; instead, the ideas of human action presented by the model are inherently impulsive. Under the view of exemplarity and imitation I have emphasized, then, much imitative action does indeed seem animalistic and irrational. It therefore seems like something that should be shunned by moral educators concerned with finding intelligent and appropriate reasons for action. This sort of imitation is an automatic response like digestion—hardly the sort of thing worthy of moral praise. At first glance, then, many imitative actions appear to be morally inferior to other sorts of reasoned action.

But is this necessarily the case? It seems to me that there is a good argument that suggests a different conclusion; namely, that imitative moral action and independently reasoned moral action can be of equal moral worth. The argument for this position, which I can only sketch here, is built on four main ideas:

1. Reasons are always based on "forms of life"—systems of communal action that serve as the ultimate basis of justification.

2. Forms of life are intimately tied to human exemplars that give access to the form of life.

3. Thus, all forms of reason are closely tied to human exemplars.

4. Thus, there is no great distance between imitative action and reasoned action.

The major sources to draw on for help in establishing the first point are the philosopher-psychologists Ludwig Wittgenstein and William James. The second point can be established with reference to the social nature of examples developed in previous chapters. The third and fourth points seem to follow as conclusions from the first two premises.

The initial point that needs to be established, then, is that human reason is ultimately based on forms of life. Although it would be impossible to independently establish this point given the limitations of this chapter, it is an idea that gained considerable currency in 20th century philosophy.[4] James and Wittgenstein, for example, are both in agreement on this issue. To the skeptic who questions the ultimate validity of knowledge claims, James and Wittgenstein argue that knowledge claims always involve interconnected systems of thought and action.[5] These systems of thought and action "hang together" and form a holistic unity. In *On Certainty*, Wittgenstein writes:

> Our knowledge forms an enormous system. And only within this system has a particular bit the value we give it. (§410)

> If I say "we *assume* that the earth has existed for many years past" (or something similar), then of course it sounds strange that we should assume such a thing. But in the entire system of our language games it belongs to the foundations. The assumption, one might say, forms the basis of action, and therefore, naturally, of thought. (§411)

Since most of our actions implicitly depend on a stable world, our actions presuppose the knowledge that the "earth has existed for many years past." The idea of a stable world is something our systems of action must take for granted for us to act in ways that we do. This echoes the sentiment Wittgenstein expresses in §204 of *On Certainty*: "Giving grounds, however, justifying the evidence, comes to an end;— but the end is not certain propositions' striking us as immediately true, i.e., it is not a kind of *seeing* on our part; it is our *acting*, which lies at the bottom of the language game."

Wittgenstein reluctantly finds that his position sounds "something like pragmatism" (§422), as well he should. James had laid the psychological basis for his pragmatism in the *Principles of Psychology* (1890), where he asserts that the mind exists for action. "It is far too little recognized how entirely the intellect is built of practical interests," he writes. "The germinal question concerning things brought for the first time before consciousness is the not theoretic 'What is that?' but the practical 'Who goes there?' or rather, as Horwicz has admirably put it, 'What is to be done?'—'*Was fang' ich an?*' " (1890, pp. 313–314). Russell Goodman has described the many other points of connection between James and Wittgenstein on this topic. Although James thinks, contrary to Wittgenstein, that these basic "forms of life" are ultimately based and justified by experience, Russell shows how James and Wittgenstein both have "a sense that not all empirical propositions, or beliefs, play the same role; and a sense of the interrelation of thought and action" (Goodman, 2002, p. 19). All reasons and justifications must refer (explicitly or implicitly) back to these forms of action. Action provides the framework in which reasons are formed.

Nicholas Burbules and Paul Smeyers (2002) sum up what this means for ethical justification with reference to Wittgenstein. Wittgenstein was famous for rejecting overarching theories and focused on specific contexts and purposes. But this did not mean that justifications were impossible. It is just that for Wittgenstein these justifications

> eventually reach an end, and he says at this stage one can only describe: "this is what we do." The form of life is the bedrock beyond which explanations cannot go—nor can a form of life be asked to justify itself, because it sets the conditions for any possible justifications. (2002, p. 252)

This is relevant to the moral status of following examples because forms of life are transmitted, in large part, through our exemplars. Human practices are generally learned through observation of models and not through explication or instruction. What we think of as moral reasoning is not an exception.

Burbules and Smeyers are correct in highlighting the importance of examples in drawing people into practices, language games, and forms of life. Indeed, this is similar to what I argue in previous chapters when I suggest that human examples play an invitational role within human practices and traditions. Exemplars play a role in the formation of communities of practice and the initiation of new members into such communities. The role of exemplarity in practices and forms of life can be shown by remembering that a practice is ultimately based on the description "this is what we do." Exemplars help to constitute what counts as "we" in this description (imitation of examples creates the sense of *we-ness* by creating similar patterns of storytelling, by constructing group boundaries, and by setting the stage for common problems) and they help set the normative standard for what "we" do. So it seems correct to say that exemplars play a key role in mediating forms of life. They are embodied representations of "what we do."

If philosophers like James and Wittgenstein are correct, then, justifications and reasons for action (including moral action) must always go back to forms of life. If we then say that forms of life are represented by examples, then it follows that justifications and reasons are also intimately tied to exemplary representations. The exemplar gives us access to forms of life that allow for justification and reasoning.

This conclusion has implications for how we evaluate the moral standing of the reason "because someone else is doing it." This reason is a description of a form of life, just as the reason "because this is what we do" is based on a description of a form of life. A description of a form of life is the basis for both types of justifications. This analysis indicates that all moral reasoning (whether explicitly based on exemplars or not) is built on a similar foundation. It blurs the distinction between independently justified actions and imitative actions. "Because someone else is doing it" can be seen as simply another way of saying, "Because this is what we do."

This is not to say that imitative action based on exemplars and independently reasoned action are equivalent in every respect—we still might prefer some distance between the descriptive statement ("someone else is doing it" or "this is what we do") and the moral action. We do not want to arrive at this statement too quickly. A degree of justificatory distance may provide room for debate and deliberation that otherwise would be foreclosed. But if all reasons for action ultimately fall back on these descriptive statements, then it seems misguided to draw a sharp differentiation in the moral status between these and other reasons for action.

In sum, I have presented several reasons to be suspicious of the idea that imitative action cannot be praiseworthy moral action. First, I have suggested that it is not entirely settled whether moral action must be based on proper intentions and justifications. Second, I have indicated that most educators who have endorsed imitative learning have suggested that reasons for imitation go beyond the reason of "someone else is doing it." Both of these suggestions, though, are ultimately unsatisfactory, at least with respect to the broad range of imitative action. Therefore, the third suggestion is the most central in answering the objection: All justifications are ultimately based on exemplars that grant access to forms of life. There is a similar justificatory basis for doing something "because someone else is doing it" and for doing something for allegedly more praiseworthy reasons.

CONCLUSION

In the above analysis of moral reason, I have tried to show that moral reasoning built around examples of human life has resources to overcome the common objections. That is, I have argued that moral reasoning, when based on examples, does not necessarily succumb to the criticisms typically laid against it. By looking at the greater social context, I have shown how exemplars can promote flexibility, creativity, and criticality. Reasoning based on exemplars is based on the same foundation as any other conception of moral reasoning, and thus may be just as worthy of moral praise or blame. None of this proves that a process of moral reason based on exemplars must necessarily be productive, flexible, and praiseworthy. In any particular instance, it could very well be the opposite. But following examples can provide an *openness* that is not at first apparent and that sometimes may equal other types of practical reasoning. The question of moral reason shows why we should look beyond the observer and the model when thinking through the educational influence of human lives.

CHAPTER 7

How Can We Evaluate
Human Exemplars?

The idea of imitating examples can evoke troubling images. We may imagine thoughtless masses of people adoring the image of a charismatic tyrant, blindly obeying his commands and following either his own example or the examples he designates. We may think of tragic cases involving mass imitation—of the Hitler Youth, Jim Jones and his followers, or the American soldiers at My Lai. Or we may think of less radical but perhaps more common instances of people believing and doing simply as everyone else does, with little critical thought. In the previous chapter, I have argued that imitation can help create an environment conducive to critical thought and that critical thought is itself built on examples that give us access to forms of life. However, when we imitate examples it still seems as though we cannot be critical about the human exemplars themselves. Even if we imitate a philosophic example by being critical, it seems that the example is still left outside of the realm of critical engagement. Imitating Socrates seems to make us critical of everything but Socrates himself. What room is there, then, for intelligent engagement with influential models? If we can, in fact, critically evaluate exemplars, then this will help us gauge the ultimate value of learning from the examples of others. In this chapter, I wish to sketch what an answer to these questions might look like.

If we take seriously what has been argued in previous chapters, it appears that a satisfactory answer to this question is even more distant than it was before. The influence of human exemplars, as it has appeared in previous chapters, has been shown to become less and less manageable. Examples influence human development in ways that often transcend our individual control. Social contexts contain markers of similarity and difference that turn things into examples, they influence the construction of self-narratives that influence the imitative response, and they involve imitative meanings that change educational environments. The standard model of imitation, which involves a rational means-to-ends selection of exemplars, seems to be only one of many ways in which exemplarity can work. Exemplars are chosen for us as much as we choose them, and we can often only recognize their influence by looking backward at the shape our lives have taken. For this reason, it is hard to see how we could be critical of the examples themselves. They will have their influence whether we want them to or not.

It is also difficult to see how we can possibly have an evaluative space that stands apart from exemplarity, a space in which rational criticism of our examples may take place. Exemplars give us access to forms of life and, if philosophers like Wittgenstein and William James are correct, forms of life are the ultimate basis for justification. It follows that there is little or no room apart from examples to formulate independent justifications for examples. As Irene Harvey (2002) has implied, our notions of critical thought are closely connected with the examples of critical reason that have been presented to us. Even if we wanted to eradicate exemplars from education in the name of critical thinking, it would probably be impossible to do so. Examples at least partially construct what it means to think critically. So it seems there is little space to critically engage with examples apart from examples.

The power to educate through example, it seems, will always be with those who have the power to shape the social world. If the powerful understand and are somehow able to harness the processes of exemplarity, such actions appear tyrannical because they function below the radar screen of critical reason. If those who are in power do not understand the processes of exemplarity, then the influence of exemplars will be haphazard and random, perhaps reflecting the values of the marketplace more than anything else. Because there seems to be little space for intelligent engagement with exemplars, they would appear to lend themselves to exploitation, whether through totalitarian regimes, big business interests, or uncritical "character education" programs.

Is there a way to critically assess exemplars while at the same time acknowledging the realities of their power and their connection to social forces beyond our control as individuals? To answer this question,

I wish to use the example of the ancient Pyrrhonian Skeptics, who advanced what seems to be an intelligent form of education, but one that did not by design go any deeper than examples of human lives. They understood the impossibility of going completely beyond examples, but they worked within these limitations toward a sort of critical engagement. The Skeptics are useful because they understood that it is impossible to determine whether an example is, in its very essence, good or bad. They would say our perception, even of other human lives, does not reveal the "real" nature of things. Our perception of examples will always be colored by other examples, and the Skeptics' awareness of these sorts of limitations makes them useful companions.

ANCIENT SKEPTICISM, EXEMPLARITY, AND CRITICALITY

The earliest representative of the skeptical tradition in philosophy is Pyrrho of Elis (c. 360–c. 270 BC). Pyrrho, we are told, once declared that all things are "equally indifferent, unmeasurable, and inarbitrable" (quoted in Long & Sedly, 1987, p. 15). From what can be gleaned from later Pyrrhonists, it seems that Pyrrho's version of ancient skepticism held that the mind has no access to things apart from sense perception, that sense perception does not guarantee that we perceive things as they really are, and that therefore there is no way to know the true nature of things. For the Skeptic, it is not given to human beings to know reality. While it may seem that such a radical philosophy would make education impossible, the Skeptics did, in fact, make claims about education. Or, more precisely, they enacted a process of education. Their system of education revolved around the imitation of examples. Examples show us how to live, even though an educator cannot offer an unshakable theoretical case for how we should live. The Skeptics, then, present a number of paradoxes. They did not believe that knowledge was possible and yet they believed in education. This is odd since education is generally thought of, at least partially, as the transmission or creation of knowledge. Further, they believed in teaching by example even though they appear to have had no way of justifying their examples. How did they resolve such inconsistencies?

   The prominent educator in the ancient skeptical tradition was Timon of Phlius (c.320–c.230 BC), a man who was greatly impressed by the presence, disposition, and emotional life of Pyrrho. He often drew attention to the life of his master Pyrrho using the most glorious language: "Truly," he proclaimed, echoing the language reserved for the hero Odysseus, "no other mortal could rival Pyrrho" (Long &

Sedley, p. 18, compare with the *Iliad*, 3:223.).[1] The fact that Timon was alluding to the Homeric tradition is telling, since many ancient educators took the heroes of Homer to be the supreme models for imitation. Timon was offering Pyrrho as a substitute for the Homeric heroes, just as Plato had offered Socrates. Pyrrho was the example that made moral education possible.

Timon mentioned the specific qualities of Pyrrho's life in numerous fragments. Aristocles quotes Timon's description of his mentor, which depicts Pyrrho's freedom from normal problems of life:

> Such was the man I saw, unconceited and unbroken by all the pressures that have subdued the famed and unfamed alike, unstable band of people, weighed down on this side and on that with passions, opinions, and futile legislation. (Long & Sedley, p. 18)

From this fragment, it is clear that Timon seems to have been deeply impressed by the tranquility and peace that he found in Pyrrho when compared to those who were stressed from the pressures of justifying their beliefs. Note also when Diogenes Laertius quotes Timon as saying:

> This, O Pyrrho, my heart yearns to hear, how on earth you, though a man, act most easily and calmly, never taking thought and consistently undisturbed, heedless of the whirling motions and sweet voice of wisdom? You alone lead the way for men, like the god who drives around the whole earth as he revolves, showing the blazing disk of his well-rounded sphere. (Long & Sedley, p. 19)

Pyrrho's biography is revealed as a godlike beacon to humanity, leading the way to a realm of an impenetrably serene existence. The example of Pyrrho's life is held up as an example for all to follow. Since Pyrrho led a life of skepticism, and since his life appeared to be peaceful, one should imitate Pyrrho's skepticism and give up the concern with always trying to be *right* about how things really are.

But, again, why should we think that the Skeptics are really right in their elevation of Pyrrho's example? How can they offer a justification for their example, if all justifications eventually fail? Critical to understanding the moral education of ancient Pyrrhonian Skeptics is the fact that, although they emphasized the suspension of judgment concerning the true nature of things, they did not deny that things *appear* to be a certain way. The later Pyrrhonists "affirm[ed] to appearance, without also affirming that is of such a kind" (Long & Sedley, p. 15). Thus, the skeptic had no trouble saying the cruel life appears

to a bad thing; they simply refused to state that it really *is* a bad t
Timon summed up the position with a useful example, "That h(
is sweet I do not affirm, but I agree that it appears so" (Long & Seaiey,
p. 15). It is possible to act on the conviction of appearances, but one
should not act fanatically, thinking that an opinion goes deeper than
one's limited experience with an example.

This type of evidence from appearances is important for the
skeptic. After all, the skeptic is unable to say that one life really is
superior to another; the lessons of how to live a life cannot be based
on deductions from an independently reasoned theoretical position.
Instead, a lesson would proceed as if it were about the sweetness of
honey. By giving students the experience of tasting honey and by
having them reflect on how things appeared to them as they had the
experience, the students might become convinced of the appearance
that honey is sweet. To affirm the apparent sweetness of honey people
do not (and should not) need an unshakeable theoretical argument—
they just need a taste. Similarly, pointing to the life of Pyrrho was
Timon's way of giving people a "taste" of skeptical life. With this
taste, someone could then decide whether or not such a life—the life
of skepticism and peace—appeared to be sweet or sour. This is, of
course, a limited pedagogy. As Julia Annas writes, the Skeptic can
"merely point to the skeptical way of life and hope we find it attractive" (1993, p. 213). It is based on appearances and forever tentative,
to be sure. But it is a coherent system of reconciling skepticism with
some sort of education.

The moral education of the Skeptics is instructive because it offers clues as to how an exemplar can be intelligently engaged. The
metaphor of "tasting" is particularly helpful when addressing this
problem. When we sample a food, we taste an example of it, not
knowing beforehand whether it will be pleasing to us or not. We do
not know if the experience will be positive until *after* it has had an
experiential influence on us. After reflecting on our experience, we can
then decide whether we want to continue eating the food or not. This
is a common way of doing things, and we would think it odd for a
judgment about food to happen any other way—it would be strange,
for example, to trust a theoretical argument "proving" which food
would be enjoyable. This same tasting method, it seems to me, can be
applied to how we intelligently engage with exemplars. We cannot
know beforehand how a human life will influence us. Even what we
consider to be bad examples may have aspects that influence us for
good, depending on what we "see" in their example (we might "see"
Gavrilo's political passion and imitate that rather than his inclination

to murder). We taste lives and bring ourselves into contact with others, we are influenced by their example, and then we decide what the influence has been and whether to continue to allow this influence. The social forces involved with exemplars often deny us a rational choice before working their influence, and we can only reflect on our experience with examples after the experiential fact.

The problem with the tasting metaphor is that concepts like "taste" are at least partially constructed through exemplarity. The sorts of foods we enjoy are influenced, for example, by who we think we are, and who we think we are is a function of exemplarity. People may come from an upper-class background and may be raised around human examples who do not eat "fast food." Examples contribute to who these people perceive themselves to be, and this will, in turn, influence the sorts of foods they enjoy. Things like taste are, in large part, a product of our positions in our cultures and traditions, and we have access to our culture at least partly by being exposed to human examples that show us our place. What holds true for judgments of taste also holds true for our other standards of judgment—what counts as good philosophy, for instance, largely has to do with the examples a young philosopher is exposed to during her education. In short, value judgments about our "own" experiences are shaped by past examples. So not even this "tasting" sort of education escapes the influences of human examples; they always lurk in the background of the judgment itself. So, once again, it appears that we cannot ground judgment in a neutral place outside of exemplarity.

What this tasting sort of education does do, however, is place the human examples in a framework so that they can be analyzed in terms of their *coherence*. An example is to be analyzed by how well it coheres with our other tastes, beliefs, and desires. This analysis of human examples does not get down to any truth about the way things really are—the standards by which we judge examples are contingent and are themselves based on examples. But it does give us a way of evaluating examples that involves a degree of intelligence. To taste an example is to make a postexperiential judgment on how the experience coheres with our other normative examples. The example under consideration is examined by the standards of judgment that are themselves based on examples. The framework of examples that constitutes the standard is held constant while the one particular example in question is evaluated.

This is often what we do when we appear to be criticizing examples on independent grounds. Suppose we were considering whether we should continue to imitate a philosophical model. We may criticize the philosopher on the grounds that he or she is "unintelligent" and "closed minded." This sort of criticism, however, is itself likely to be based on our exemplars. Indeed, our understanding of concepts like "intelligent" and "open minded" probably involve human examples of such traits from our experience. As we criticize the philosopher's example, we hold these other examples constant and use them to judge the particular example in question.

It is important to note that this skeptical, "tasting" sort of analysis appears to skirt the need to make statements that are either true or false (in the sense of truth as a correspondence between ideas and reality), which is exactly what the Pyrrhonian Skeptics need to do. Their position on this point is not so different from what others have said. Consider what happens if we translate this view into the terminology of someone like Thomas Kuhn (1962): Pyrrho's life becomes something of a paradigmatic achievement, similar to the Newtonian achievements that set the stage for subsequent science. Pyrrho's life provides a model way of living to a particular community. According to Kuhn, however, scientific practitioners cannot justify the adoption of one paradigm over another purely on the basis of belief that the new paradigm is "truer" than the old one. That is, the new paradigm cannot be justified on the grounds that it is a truer picture of the way things really are. After all, what counts as true is internal to the paradigm itself. The fact that truth cannot be a factor in adopting new paradigms, for Kuhn, does not mean that new paradigms are not adopted in an intelligent way. It only means that new paradigms are adopted on grounds other than on truth or falsity. Often paradigms are adopted because of their coherence with aspects of social and psychological reality outside of scientific inquiry.

This coherence model of judging exemplars is something the pragmatic tradition in philosophy would also endorse. Using arguments from the relativity of perception that would have been at home with the ancient Skeptics, Richard Rorty makes a claim about the shift from one "vocabulary" to another. He writes: "To accept the claims that there is no standpoint outside the particular historically conditioned and temporary vocabulary we are presently using from which to judge this vocabulary is to give up on the idea that there can be reasons for using languages as well as reasons within languages for believing statements" (1989, pp. 48–49). The Skeptics would have recognized that the same doubts about an exterior standard of truth that Rorty expresses for "vocabularies" can also be applied to exemplars. And, like Rorty and Kuhn, the Skeptics suggest that a moral paradigm or vocabulary can be critically engaged, but without reference to a

grounded exterior standard. The standard to be used is
~~~~e. This position is contested, to be sure, but the idea of a
neutral ground apart from examples being necessary for intelligent
evaluation can no longer simply be taken for granted.

So how, then, do we evaluate examples? The value of examples
should be judged by what they allow us to do in the framework of
other important examples. A particular example, in other words, is
judged in terms of its coherence within a form of life. Catherine Elgin
argues that examples have little to do with "justified true belief." They
are neither true nor false and, therefore, "justification in the sense of
argument from accepted premises is out of place." Instead, an example should be judged "not by what backs it up, but by what it
brings forward" (1991, p. 207). When an example is offered, according
to Elgin, it can be more or less effective in communicating a feature,
but there is nothing true or false about it until it is described in propositions. Although the vaunted description of Pyrrho's life was done in
propositions (e.g., "no other mortal could rival Pyrrho"), the example
itself would not be something that is true or false. The example of
Pyrrho is valuable if it brings forward something important about
human lives, that is, if it allows us to live in ways that were closed off
before the example granted us its epistemic access.

THE TURN TO PRACTICES AND EXEMPLAR ROTATION

So far, I have argued that human exemplars allow for an experimental,
"tasting" form of critical analysis. After experience with a human
exemplar, it is possible to ask what the exemplar has brought forward
within the particular system of exemplarity that is of value to human
life. It is in the light of these points, I believe, that we should understand the Skeptics' other suggestions, which include a turn to existing
customs and practices. Sextus Empiricus (ca. 200 AD), a later Pyrrhonian
philosopher, writes, "For we follow a line of reasoning which, in ac-
cordance with appearances, points us to a life conformable to the
customs of our country and its laws and institutions, and to our own
instinctive feelings" (*Outlines of Pyrrhonism*, VIII, cited in Hallie, 1964,
p. 37). His emphasis on this point is stated elsewhere, when he boasts,
"Our life . . . is unprejudiced by opinions. We simply follow the laws
and customs and our natural feelings" (p. 96).

It is possible to interpret this turn to existing customs and laws
as a weak and desperate attempt to bring a practical coherence to the
skeptical life. I doubt, however, that the Skeptics take this position

Cultural relativism

merely because they lack anything better to say; instead, they take this position because it fits together with the emphasis on educational exemplification. Practices are forms of life that we access through exemplarity, and the individual is to engage actively with the full set of exemplified human practices. This active engagement is revealed when Sextus Empiricus writes:

> By the handing down of customs and laws, we accept, from an everyday point of view, that piety is good and impiety bad. By teaching of kinds of expertise we are not inactive in those of them which we accept. And we say all this without holding any opinions. (Hallie, p. 40)

As Sextus points out, the Skeptics are open to the experience of any practice or expertise that is taught in a culture—horsemanship, navigation, thievery, and so forth—but they are not "inactive" in choosing among these practices. Nor would they be inactive in choosing among the wide varieties of examples that arise in these practices. These examples are tasteable, even though they are themselves neither true nor false. The Skeptic points to the customs and the various practices within a culture as a storehouse of possible examples and encourages the student to reflect experientially on these examples. All this can be done without stating an opinion that any example is really true or false, good or bad.

The turn to existing practices, however, is troubling in several ways. If students follow the examples embedded in existing practices, and if these practices subsequently appear desirable to the students, it appears that they are unfortunately bound by a rather rigid conservatism. Teaching by example in this way will be reproductive of existing social standards; that is, it will preserve the status quo. The forms of life, the systems of exemplarity that happen to surround us, are taken as the limit of possibilities. The collection of existing examples within practices is the normative standard; they are held constant as individual examples within the system are criticized. So even if individual examples may be criticized in terms of coherence, the standard by which each individual example is judged seems to remain untouched. There is no possibility for social change or self-creation.

Now, it is true that we can criticize only one example at a time. Criticism of an example is possible because we can hold constant the other examples that help to constitute our sense of taste, our beliefs, and our standards of judgment. We can, however, shift our attention from one example to another. At one moment, a first example may serve as part of the standard by which we judge a second example. In the next moment, the first example may be criticized, while the second is held constant as part of the normative standard. When judging an example on the basis of coherence, it is essential that there be a rotation between those examples that constitute the standard for judgment and those that are being judged.

To take the metaphor of "tasting" again, we might think of human life as a wine-tasting party in which every possible wine is being sampled. At any given moment, a single wine is being tasted, while the rest of the samples are being held constant to construct the standard of judgment. The individual wine may be judged as good or bad when compared with the standard. As people sample through the selections, though, each wine will be placed in the position of being judged and in being part of the standard for judgment. Each wine helps to constitute the standard, but it will also be criticized in terms of that standard it helps to form. In situations like these, there is no standard outside the wine selections themselves. But we can advance criticisms of individual wines as the standard is brought to bear on particular samples. More importantly, though, the criticism of the samples, over time, allows for criticism and change of the standard itself. Indeed, it would even be possible to select qualities of individual wines that we admire and combine them in a new standard. This new standard would still be based on examples, but not on any one particular example.

This analogy is helpful in understanding how we might engage critically with human examples, while at the same time acknowledging their deep conceptual influence. The analogy would call for experimentation and sampling of various examples of human lives (in person or vicariously through literature, theater, and film). The examples of human lives should shift between serving as the standards of judgment and the objects of judgment. The experiences we then have are judged on the ever-shifting criterion of coherence. This experimentation with practices and examples gives the idea of "learning from example" some degree of needed flexibility. It allows for us to criticize existing standards in society and in ourselves. It makes possible a form (albeit, perhaps, a limited form) of self-creation and social flexibility.

What, no examples ?!

A CRITICAL EDUCATION AND EXEMPLARITY: A CONCLUSION

Learning from the examples of other human lives, then, allows for a sort of critical engagement. It permits criticism and creative interaction with the examples themselves. The critical engagement, however, is of a specific kind. It is a critical engagement that works within the existing social forces and systems of exemplars, rather than presuming to stand outside of them. Bringing together the major points in this and the proceeding chapters provides hints at what a critical education based on examples would look like. When thinking about human exemplars in human development and their relationship to critical thinking, I suggest we remember five important points.

First, it is essential that we not confuse examples that are taken and imitated in an uncritical and uncreative way with what learning from examples must necessarily be. Indeed, critical reason may itself be something that is modeled—something that Plato realized as he offered Socrates as his new hero. An education that aims to help students think critically is often involved in deep ways with examples of critical thinking. It is not the idea of learning from examples itself that should be interrogated if we want to foster critical thinking; rather, it is the *type* of example that should be interrogated.

Second, we should realize that critical reason is not something to locate solely in an individual mind, but in larger social groups (see chapters 5 and 6). So while any individual imitative act may appear to be unthinking and uncritical, it may be part of a larger community that is itself very critical. Rather than looking at the product of individuals, then, it is important to also look at the product of communities. Again, it is the *type* of imitation and exemplarity that is important.

Third, although it is impossible to escape exemplarity, it is possible to offer intelligent criticisms of examples. The social nature of exemplarity reveals that the processes involved with whom we take as examples (discussed in chapter 3) and whom we begin to imitate (discussed in chapter 4) are not often subject to individual preexperiential choice. Rather, the critical engagement with examples often comes *after* the example has already had an influence and provoked imitation. The type of critique that is possible (at least with many forms of examples) can come only while one is already under the influence of examples. We can work within these forces, but not step outside them.

Fourth, the intelligent engagement that is possible with examples ultimately takes the form of an analysis of coherence. That is, we judge examples based on their coherence with the other normative examples of human life. Since we cannot escape examples or the forms of life that examples give us access to, the focus of concern should be on how well one example fits together with other examples within the form of life. Of course, this is not necessarily what the criticisms of examples will explicitly look like in practice. We may be asking whether an example is good to follow, but in conceptualizing "goodness" we will necessarily be thinking in terms of examples. We analyze examples in terms of coherence, even though it may not appear to be what we are doing.

Fifth, in order to avoid a troubling conservatism, an intelligent critique of exemplars will involve an experimental approach. It will involve tasting multiple examples, reflecting on the subsequent experiences, and analyzing the exemplar for coherence with other important examples in our form of life. Each exemplar that gives us access to the standards involved with a form of life must also eventually take its places as the object of our criticism. Exemplar critique is, in this sense, a process of endless rotation.

CHAPTER 8

A Social Analysis of
Exemplarity and Imitation *nice*

Within the phenomenon of learning by example, there exists a complex interaction between individuals and larger social forces. Social conventions and structures of similarity and difference are necessary to direct our attention to things *as* examples of something. Before we are able to imitate what we see, these structures of exemplarity inform us of what it is that we are seeing. The imitative response often is an automatic result of already impulsive ideas being unleashed in action without any conscious decision to imitate. These are ideas that seem to have been sorted as "not inconsistent" with our narrative sense of self, and this narrative sense of self is a deeply social product. In addition, assessing the meaning and value of following an example also requires a larger social analysis. Within community contexts, imitation possesses powerful social meanings. Indeed, it is partly through imitation that we connect ourselves to the groups, communities, and traditions that make creative and critical activity possible and valuable.

This book has argued for a change of focus away from an individualistic way of understanding human examples (as manifest in both the standard model and its Enlightenment critics) and toward a wider social analysis. When traditional theorists of education and human development have discussed human exemplars and imitation, they generally underestimate the power of social contexts and structures that go beyond the individual exemplar and the individual learner. In some ways, of course, it has always been obvious that the social world is important to human exemplarity; indeed, the term "role

139

model" already betrays a connection to the social world because a "role" is a set of expectations present in larger social contexts. The penetration of the social world, however, goes much deeper than this. There are forces within social contexts that influence how examples are formulated, how they bring forth imitation, what imitation entails, and what imitative action means across different social contexts.

The change of focus might be clarified with an analogy to something like unemployment. To understand employment, one may first be tempted to look at individual interactions between job seekers and prospective employers. Under this type of analysis, we would look at the characteristics of the job seekers and the needs of individual employers, and we would understand unemployment as a sum total of the individual relationships between prospective employers and job seekers. It seems obvious, though, that to really understand unemployment we need to look beyond the interactions of individual job seekers and employers. There are a multitude of social forces that influence the relationship of employment: global, national, and local economic policies, community histories of sexism and racism, technological advances, and so forth. Any deep understanding of unemployment must take such factors into account. The exemplarity relationship, I contend, is similarly dependent on larger social forces, and attending to these forces increases our understanding of human development.

To show what this social analysis produces, consider the case of the medical students discussed in the first chapter. The problem, as it was described there, is the disparity between the people that the students designate as their models of good physicians and the people that they actually seem to imitate. Although students talk about wanting to be like the humane, people-oriented physicians, their imitation often seems geared toward powerful, status-oriented physicians. Perhaps the people-oriented physicians were indeed examples of some sort for the medical students, but they do not appear to be examples in the sense of being normative exemplars and future selves, that point to a process of development yet to come. Why not?

The social analysis developed in this book presents several possibilities. If the analysis of exemplarity processes I have presented is correct, one could posit that the social context is such that the students' attention is not focused on the people-oriented physicians in the proper sort of way. The context may encourage students to ignore the quiet actions of people-oriented physicians. The students may be stressed or focused on the medical problem at hand, and are therefore not really able to see the attending physician's admirable bedside manner. The attending physician's interaction with a patient is framed

as an example of solving the technical medical problem, pe
not as an example of good bedside manner—they are seeing, —
were, the ambiguous drawing as the duck and not the rabbit. One
might also posit that, although the medical students know that they
admire people-oriented physicians, these physicians' lives are not
framed so as to be seen as an example of a future self. The surrounding framework of similarity and difference is not tuned, one might say,
to that particular frequency of exemplarity. Even if there are people-
oriented physicians on a medical school faculty, the mere presence of
such people within the social context is not enough to ensure that they
will have any particular exemplary effect.

An understanding of the social nature of exemplification suggests how this exemplary disconnect can be solved. It first suggests
that educating by example depends on communities and institutions,
not just on individual teachers and learners. The task of the community is to undertake a process of *alignment*. That is, the medical education community should be concerned with aligning its moral, ethical,
and creative standards with the exemplarity processes of cultural convention and differentiation. The goal of the community should be to
organize the environment so that those who embody the desired ethical standards also catch the attention of learners in productive ways.
Things need to be arranged so that the people-oriented physicians
become examples of morally desirable characteristics.

What sometimes happens in social groups is that the markers of
difference point in a direction that is at odds with ethics and humane
action. What are these differentiating markers? Status symbols, those traditional and highly visible constituents of similarity and difference in
social contexts, are one type of prominent markers. Money and position
matter a great deal in the processes of exemplarity. As Albert Bandura
writes, "It has been abundantly documented in social-psychological research that models who are high in prestige, power, intelligence, and
competence are emulated to a considerably greater degree than models of
subordinate standing" (1971, p. 54). These status markers focus attention
on certain people and away from others, or on certain traits one person
possesses and away from other traits. These sorts of markers point away
from the people-oriented physicians and their actions; attention is drawn
toward seeing medical practice as a status-oriented affair. To teach good
medicine by example requires that such disalignments be remedied.
The people-oriented physicians need to receive markers that focus attention in their direction—perhaps through increased visibility, honors,
or material rewards. This is a problem on the community level, and it
is therefore up to the community to find a solution.

The principle holds true for institutions that may wish to offer role models to help advance minority groups within their student populations through the use of minority role models. It seems that inclusion within a faculty of people who are representative of minority populations is not, by itself, sufficient for exemplarity to occur. The status markers that are salient factors in constructing similarity and difference must also be in line with the desired exemplification.

It is also helpful to consider the problem of medical school in terms of the narrative-self theory of imitation. According to this theory, developed in chapter 4 with the help of William James's ideomotor theory of action, all ideas are impulsive and those impulsive ideas that are enacted are those that are not inconsistent with the narrative sense of self. This theory would see the lack of people-oriented imitation as stemming from two main causes: (a) there is a lack of impulsive ideas from which to draw out imitation, (b) an impulsive idea is being rejected by a competing idea, often stemming from the sense of self. If we follow the first causal suggestion we may conclude that there are simply not enough examples of people-oriented physicians in medical schools to draw out observable imitation in students. If we follow the second suggestion, it may be that there is lack of fit between the examples offered by people-oriented physicians and the life narratives of the medical students. Or alternatively, the problem may be a particularly strong *coherence* between the life narratives of the medical students and the examples of the status-oriented physicians rather than that of the people-oriented physicians.

The last alternative has more prima facie appeal. It is probably not so much that the people-oriented representations of medical practice conflict with the students' sense of themselves; rather, it is that the status-oriented representations find a much stronger positive connection. I have already pointed out that we do not construct a life story on our own. Our stories are constructed with the help of larger cultural forces and narratives. In Western societies, at least, stories of a successful life are often framed in terms of salary, prestige, and status (think of "rags to riches" stories). Our own individual stories often reflect this cultural inheritance. In the context of medical education, the lives of status-oriented physicians fit in well with the general character of these larger success narratives, and they therefore will be highly influential. A strong positive connection will be created between the example of the status-oriented physician and the life narratives of the medical students, and this connection will create a strong imitative response. Thus, a Jamesian diagnosis of the problem suggests that the student life narratives, inclined by social influence to value power and privilege, are not properly impeding the ideas of status orientation from being expressed in action.

A pedagogy that took seriously the social aspects of selves, and therefore of imitation, would focus on the development of the young physicians' life stories. Once the individual narratives are built around the ideals of people-oriented practice, then the narrative sense of self will find more tension with the status-orientated examples. That is, the sense of self will serve as a "conflicting idea" that inhibits the impulsive ideas of the status-oriented examples from being acted upon.

Suppose that the community is successful and the medical students began to imitate the positive, people-oriented role models of medical practice. What are we to think of the fact that their actions are imitative? Might that itself be an impediment to proper medical practice in a changing world? After all, the idea of what constitutes humane medicine is likely to change. Under the social analysis of imitation, we recognize that imitation need not be negatively evaluated in its ability to facilitate practical reasoning. If imitation forms a community where inquiry takes place, and if imitation is centered on processes of reflective action rather than on the resulting products, then imitation may be just what is needed in a changing world. A major point of medical education should involve infusing role-model relationships with visible processes of deliberation. The role model should be not only to be seen acting, but also thinking aloud about problems, talking to others about problems, and consulting research and scholarship. By encouraging imitative deliberation, the models show that part of medical practice is reflecting intelligently on that practice. Medical education should also encourage a wide variety of possible models, thus allowing for processes of exemplar rotation that allow for some degree of criticism of the exemplars themselves, even the deliberative examples.

A social analysis of human exemplarity and imitation also has much to add to the debate surrounding media violence. The social analysis of imitation offers clues that address some of the quandaries I discussed in the first chapter—questions of why different instances of observed violence, for example, have such different imitative outcomes. Some violent actions are framed (through the processes of exemplarity) in a way that turns the actions into examples of possible future selves, while other actions are not framed in this way. Some violent actions may also speak to social and individual narratives, and therefore be more likely to elicit an imitative response.

The social analysis of learning by example helps to clarify the dilemma of media violence. As I indicated earlier, there are many justifiable, research-based reasons to be concerned about media violence. But there are also several ways in which we might act so that violent representations are not expressed in practice. First, there are the processes of exemplarity by which we categorize the representation. Second, as Dijksterhuis (2005) has pointed out, a representation of violence might not be imitated if the observer is placed in a context that focuses on self-reflection rather than on being engrossed in the exterior environment. Finally, the represented action may be deemed inconsistent with the narrative sense of self, and therefore, be held in check and not imitated.

These buffers suggest many ways in which we might deal with media violence. A community should attempt to shift the processes of exemplification toward categorizing violent actions as "immoral" or "weak" and away from being classified as "heroic," "courageous," or "manly." If educators know that children are exposed to violent media, for example, they may want to try to reframe violence by creating a Plutarch-like group of comparison where one element of media reinterprets the another (the *Diary of Anne Frank*, which discusses violence from a victim's point of view, could serve to reinterpret a positive representation of violence in a popular film). Another way to counteract violent media would be for a social group to increase the amount of self-reflection by encouraging practices that promote exploration of the self (journal keeping, for instance). If current research is correct, deep habits of self-reflection may very well break the imitative spell of violent media. Finally, a community should work to change its collective self-narratives away from those that might be consistent with glorifying violence. The violent act would then be rejected as being inconsistent with the narrative sense of self.

The advantage of looking at media violence in this way is that it acknowledges the real power that human examples can have while avoiding the conclusion that strict censorship is necessary. This point was made in chapter 4 when the narrative theory of imitation was discussed, but it applies to the other chapters as well. There are ways of dealing with media violence that do not involve its complete suppression—as I pointed out earlier, complete elimination is not viable or even desirable from an educational standpoint.

The disadvantage of looking at media violence in this way is that it seems to demand an intrusive educational hand. The idea of aligning community markers with larger community ideals and of trying to influence the narrative identities of students may perhaps seem unjustified in liberal democratic societies. In reality, though, these sorts of activities are not as intrusive as they might seem at first, at least no more than common educational practices. After all, insisting that so-cial markers are arranged so as to cohere with a community's ideals hardly seems like a radical idea as long as those ideals themselves are nonrepressive and nondiscrimatory. Further, education has always been about changing or refining an individual's identity. Even the staunch-est liberal defenders of supposedly neutral "values clarification" pro-grams, it has been shown, seem to be imparting a sense of value to students, even as they deny they are doing so (see Gutmann, 1987, pp. 54–56). If education cannot involve some change of identity, some change in life narratives, then education is impossible. It seems that educating against violence in this way does not seem any more intru-sive than any other sort of education. A community may therefore work to solve these problems of imitative violence.

Looking beyond the qualities of the individual model and ob-server, then, supports different ways of approaching problems related to human learning. This approach suggests promising proposals for how we think about the environment surrounding human develop-ment. When studying imitation and human exemplarity, it is useful to turn away from the individual human subject and toward the prac-tices, communities, and traditions in which the individual is situated.

Without a larger social view, it is impossible to fully comprehend how examples are created and how they bring about imitation. It is impossible to understand the many ways in which "following an ex-ample" shapes educational environments. It is impossible to find the proper place of examples in mature moral reason, to know how to deal with the presence of bad examples, and to grasp the intricacies of teaching through example. This social critique of human exemplarity offers new possibilities in rethinking educational practice and offers insights into how we can be influenced by exemplars, yet still interact with them in creative and critical ways. Without an appreciation of the social context of imitation, we will be unable understand how one life can transform another.

Notes

CHAPTER 2. THE HISTORICAL TRADITION OF HUMAN EXEMPLARITY

1. Unless otherwise noted, Classical sources will be cited using line, paragraph, or section numbering.

2. See, for example, 2 Thess. 3:6–13 and 1 Peter 3:5–6. The Apostle Paul saw imitation of Jesus' life and death through ritual (e.g., through baptism) as participating in his redeeming life, and hence, as an essential feature of Christian thought. New Testament writers drew heavily on the tradition of Greco-Roman moral exhortation, of which the imitation of exemplars was a prominent feature. The idea of exemplification as invitation and participation will play an important role in later chapters.

3. Jaeger discusses the middle Latin term, *documentum*. A "document" in today's world is a text, but in the Middle Ages the *documentum* could also be the example of the master. The example was a text to be studied. Thus, as Jaeger says, the Middle Ages involved a "blurring of the borders between physical presence of a teacher and the contents of a lesson" (1994, p. 12).

4. In spite of such language, recent commentators on Kant believe they have found room in his moral philosophy for experience and legitimate social influence. See especially Barbara Herman's work (1993).

5. Gelley (1995) summarizes Kant's position in the *Critique of Judgment*: "Kant argues that what is truly exemplary in genius is what cannot be imitated, the manifestation of artistic freedom, the capacity to fashion 'a new rule for art,' one that implicitly demolishes the exemplary instance, the prior rule" (CJ, §49) (1998, p. 329, footnote 21).

6. For example, see Isocrates' letter to Phillip:

> I believe I can convince you by many examples that it will also be easy for you to do this. For if it can be shown that other men in the past have undertaken enterprises which were not, indeed, more noble or more righteous than that which I have advised, but of greater magnitude and difficulty, and have actually brought them to pass, what ground will be left to my opponents to argue that you will not accomplish the easier task more quickly than other men the harder? ("Letter to Phillip," 56–59)

147

In this passage, Isocrates is not urging Phillip to imitate examples of the past. By remembering the great things others have done, Phillip will gain inspiration and the necessary social validation to accomplish his own, easier goals.

7. For example, see Plutarch:

> And though I do not think that perverting of some to secure the setting of others very humane, or a good civil policy, still when men have led reckless lives . . . perhaps it will not be much amiss for me to introduce a pair or two of them into my biographies, though not that I may merely divert and amuse my readers by giving variety to my writing. . . . Antigenidas [a composer] used to think that young men would listen with more pleasure to good flute players if they were given an experience of bad ones. (Malherbe, 1986, pp. 137–138)

Although Plutarch is still writing in a framework of imitation, in this passage, he seems to recognize that examples (in this case, bad examples) can sculpt our sensibilities and therefore that imitation does not exhaust how we learn from examples.

8. Lloyd Morgan (1896) insightfully distinguished this sort of intelligent imitation, which is based on experience and satisfaction, from more "instinctive" types of imitation that operate independent of experience.

CHAPTER 3. HOW DO PEOPLE BECOME EXAMPLES?

1. As Arrell (1990) points out, there are several possible problems with this view. First, it seems to imply that something that we have no name or symbol for (e.g., a particular shade of blue) cannot be exemplified. Second, it implies a linkage between the object and the label. Third, it seems to invalidate our experience of art—we do not perceive that a piece of music refers to the predicate "joyful"; rather, we seem to "perceive the joyfulness directly" (p. 236). Arrell instead suggests that examples constrain the categories we apply to an object. In his view, the music constrains us to perceive it as joyful. For my purposes in this chapter, however, the differences between Arrell and Goodman are relatively unimportant.

2. This process could be called "mimetic engineering" and has been discussed in a context of terrorism by Pech (2003). Pech argues that rethinking the labels that media sources use to discuss terrorism might inhibit imitative terrorism. Such a strategy would make sense if it changes the processes of exemplification. Relabeling certain actions may be part of rearranging the context of meaning surrounding specific actions.

3. To make this last point, Lucian brings Peregrinus into another comparison group with the Brahmans. In this group, the Brahmans exemplify

strength in fiery death; Peregrinus comes off as not exemplifying this trait. There may exist, then, comparison groups within comparison groups as the author tries to reinterpret the example.

CHAPTER 4. HOW DO EXAMPLES BRING OUT IMITATION?

1. The psychoanalytic approach to imitation is similar in some ways to René Girard's approach to mimetic desire. Imitation or mimesis is born out of a desire to complete oneself in another. For a discussion of Girard and imitation, see Livingston (1992).

2. Meltzoff's claim, although widely accepted, is not without its critics. Heyes (2001) argues, "Tongue protrusion is the only gesture for which there is reliable evidence that observation increases the frequency of subsequent performance in neonates" (p. 253). Further, "If tongue protrusion is the only body movement that newborns can imitate, it is plausible that the mediating process is an innate releasing mechanism, an inborn stimulus-response link, wherein the response coincidentally resembles the stimulus from a third-party perspective" (p. 253).

Thus, the tongue protrusions are not imitative, but more like a reflex action (like getting tapped on the knee with a hammer) and only accidentally looks like imitation. Heyes advances a more experiential model of imitation than does Meltzoff: Imitative reactions are learned by experiential pairing of observation and action. Whoever eventually turns out to be right in this debate, however, will make little difference for my claims in this chapter. My thesis only needs to stipulate the close connection between action and perception. I have no particular stake in whether this link is innate or learned. See also Anisfeld (2005).

3. Other nueroscientific research in support of the narrative self is found in Gallagher (2003).

4. Tan (1995) offers an opposing view, as do Canes and Rosen (1995).

5. It may be the case that a lack of these "enabling conditions" may reduce to simply forming an antagonistic representation. That is, the perception of a lack of a pedestrian to save may form an antagonistic representation that inhibits the imitative action.

6. After reviewing the literature on imitation and the justifications for free speech, Susan Hurley (2006) presents an impressive overall argument that violent entertainment should not, in fact, be considered "protected speech." The specific view of violent entertainment adopted in the argument may be a bit shallow, though, as it dismisses the democratic and educational possibilities of violent media. This view also needs to take more seriously the connection between exemplification and imitation—we do not always see violent media in a straightforward way (see chapter 3).

7. In chapter 8, I point out that another way to accommodate the existence of violent media with concerns about imitation has to do with the idea

of "self-focus" as proposed by Ap Dijksterhuis (2005). People are less likely to exhibit imitative behavior when the focus of attention shifts away from the model to the self. If this is true, it seems that one strategy of working for nonviolence involves helping students to acquire habits that involve self-reflection. If students are encouraged to write about what they experience in mass media as it relates to their own lives (for example, in journals, diaries, or weblogs), then these sorts of practices will work to increase the degree of "self focus" and draw attentional resources away from violent or troubling representations of human action.

CHAPTER 5. THE SOCIAL MEANINGS OF IMITATION

1. Although this chapter will focus on the meanings of human exemplarity as they relate to imitation (that is, to "following an example"), there are other ways in which human exemplarity has acquired meaning. The activity of "being an example," for instance, has often been thought to be meaningful in educational thought. Most often in educational writings, the human exemplar is taken as evidence or proof of a certain doctrine, or as an incarnation of words "in the flesh." These types of exemplary meanings, which relate exemplars to their professed doctrines, also deserve consideration and criticism.

2. As with flattery, a model's reaction to imitation will depend upon the attributions made about the imitator and the perceived motivations for the imitation. For example, research indicates that if the model construes that the person is imitating in order to curry favor, then the model will react negatively. Other factors mentioned by Thelen and colleagues (1981) include whether the model feels constrained in her action by being imitated and whether she considers the imitator to be incompetent. Both factors will elicit a more negative response from the model.

3. Kelman (1961) makes a related point in his work on identification, where an individual begins to assume the attitudes and actions of the identified group. For Kelman, identification happens because the individual wants to maintain a relationship to the identified group.

4. There are human examples that do not involve imitation but that, like imitated examples, mediate community membership. For instance, a human example may mediate group membership by posing a common question to a community, rather than stimulating collective imitative action. An example may also be the object of worship; it may stimulate collective action but not in any imitative way. This community-mediation feature of nonimitative exemplars also needs to be more fully explored.

5. The model-obstacle dynamic is discussed at great length by Livingston (1992).

6. One study (Thelen & Kirkland, 1976) found that children were more attracted to imitators who were older than themselves. Age and its related status for children, in this instance, influenced the meaning the imitation was taken to

have. Roberts (1980) showed that the perceived "competence" of the imitator was an important factor in some ways (increasing "reciprocal imitation"), but it did not increase affection in the same way. Rosen, Musser, and Brown (2002–2003) show that gender also matters to how imitation is interpreted.

7. Rosen, Musser, and Brown (2002–2003) point out that most research showing a positive response to being imitated has been done with actions that were instrumental. They suggest that imitating ends or actions of "intrinsic" worth may be different.

8. I discuss the distinction between "process imitation" and "product imitation" in greater depth in the next chapter.

9. Information about the Globe Program can be found at: http://www.globe.gov/globe_flash.html.

CHAPTER 6. IMITATION, EXEMPLARITY, AND MORAL REASON

1. This is the problem of the "accordion effect," which I discussed in early chapters using the example of Gavrilo Principi. Where Erde thinks a theory is necessary to focus observation on relevant aspects of actions, I have described this problem in terms of processes of exemplification.

2. This is perhaps what Albert Bandura means when he writes:

> Modeled activities thus convey principles for generative and innovative behavior. In abstract observational learning, observers extract the principles or standards embodied in the thinking and actions exhibited by others. Once they acquire the principles, they can use them to generate new instances of behavior that go beyond what they have seen, read, or heard. (2003, p. 169)

Bandura should probably qualify these sentences—modeled activities can convey principles for generative behavior but do not always do so. His basic point, though, is correct.

3. The pragmatist tradition in philosophy has gone a long way in showing how ends and means are always simultaneously critiqued (or, at least, always *should* be simultaneously critiqued). It seems, then, that this attack on the standard model is not ultimately defeated on these grounds.

4. This is a resurrection of many ideas from Ancient Greek philosophy, most notably, from Aristotle.

5. I am indebted to Goodman (2002) for calling attention to this passage and for alerting me to the connection between James and Wittgenstein on this point.

References

Anderson, C. A., & Bushman, B. J. (2002). The effects of media violence of society. *Science, 295*, 2377–2379.

Anisfeld, M. (2005). No compelling evidence to dispute Piaget's timetable of the development of representational imitation in infancy. In S. Hurley & N. Chater (Eds.), *Perspectives on imitation: From neuroscience to social science, volume 2* (pp. 107–132). Cambridge, MA: MIT Press.

Annas, J. (1993). *The morality of happiness.* New York: Oxford University Press.

Arrell, D. (1990). Exemplification reconsidered. *British Journal of Aesthetics, 30* (3), 233– 243.

Ashworth, J., & Evans, J. L. (2001). Modeling student subject choice at secondary and tertiary level: A cross-section study. *Journal of Economic Education, 32* (4), 311–320.

Augustine (1948 version). *The basic writings of Saint Augustine.* New York: Random House.

Bandura, A. (1971). Analysis of modeling process. In Albert Bandura (Ed.) *Psychological modeling: Conflicting theories* (pp. 1–63). Chicago, IL: Aldine-Atherton.

Bandura, A. (1986). *Social foundations of thought and action: A social cognitive theory.* Englewood Cliffs, NJ: Prentice-Hall.

Bandura, A. (2003). On the psychosocial impact and mechanisms of spiritual modeling. *The International Journal for the Psychology of Religion, 13* (3), 167–173.

Bandura, A., Ross, D., & Ross, S. A. (1961). Transmission of aggression through imitation of aggressive models. *Journal of Abnormal and Social Psychology, 63*, 575–582.

Bandura, A., & Walters, R. H. (1963). *Social learning and personality development.* New York: Holt, Rinehart & Winston.

Bargh, J. A., Chen, M., & Burrows, L. (1996). Automaticity in social behavior: Direct effects of trait construct and stereotype activation. *Journal of Personality and Social Psychology, 71*, 230–244.

Barton, J. (1998). Approaches to ethics in the Old Testament. In J. Rogerson (Ed.), *Beginning Old Testament study*. St. Louis, MO: Chalice.

Bickle, J. (2003). Empirical evidence for a narrative concept of self. In G. D. Fireman, T. E. McVay, Jr., & O. Flanagan (Eds.), *Narrative and consciousness: Literature, psychology, and the brain* (pp. 195–208). New York: Oxford University Press.

Bruner, J. (2003). Self-making narratives. In R. Fivush & C. A. Haden (Eds.), *Autobiographical memory and the construction of a narrative self* (pp. 209–225). Mahwah, NJ: Erlbaum.

Burbules, N. C., & Smeyers, P. (2002). Wittgenstein, the practice of ethics, and moral education. *Philosophy of Education, 2002*. Urbana, IL: Philosophy of Education Society.

Bushman, B. J., & Anderson, C. A. (2001). Media violence and the American public: Scientific facts versus media misinformation. *American Psychologist, 56* (6/7), 477–489.

Canes, B. J., & Rosen, H. S. (1995). Following in her footsteps? Women's choices of college majors and faculty gender composition. *Industrial and Labor Relations, 48* (3), 486–504.

Carlyle, T. (1841/1904). *On heroes, hero-worship and the heroic in history*. New York: Scribner.

Carver, C. S., Ganellen, R. J., Froming, W. J., & Chambers, W. (1983). Modeling: An analysis in terms of category accessibility. *Journal of Experimental Social Psychology, 19*, 403–421.

Chartrand, T. L., & Bargh, J. A. (1999). The chameleon effect: The perception-behavior link and social interaction. *Journal of Personality and Social Psychology, 76* (6), 893–910.

Dabbs, J. M. (1969). Similarity of gesture and interpersonal influence. *Proceedings of the 77th*[th] *Annual Convention of the American Psychological Association, 4*, 337–338.

Dautenhahn, K., & Nehaniv, C. L. (Eds.) (2002a). *Imitation in animals and artifacts*. Cambridge, MA: MIT Press.

Dautenhahn, K., & Nehaniv, C. L. (2002b). The agent-based perspective on imitation. In K. Dautenhahn and C. L. Nehaniv (Eds.), *Imitation in animals and artifacts* (pp. 1–40). Cambridge, MA: MIT Press.

Decety, J. (2002). Is there such a thing as functional equivalence between imagined, observed, and executed action? In A. N Meltzoff and W. Prinz (Eds.), *The imitative mind: Development, evolution, and brain bases* (pp. 291–310). New York: Cambridge University Press.

Decety, J., Grèzes, J., Costes, N., Perani, D., Jeannerod, M., Procyk, E., Grassi, F., & Fazio, F. (1997). Brain activity during observation of actions: Influence of action content and subject's strategy. *Brain, 120*, 1763–1777.

Dennett, D. C. (1992) The self as a center of narrative gravity. In F. Kessel, P. Cole, and D. Johnson (Eds.), *Self and consciousness: Multiple perspectives.* Hillsdale, NJ: Erlbaum.

Dijksterhuis, A. (2005). Why we are social animals: The high road to imitation as social glue. In S. Hurley & N. Chater (Eds.), *Perspectives on imitation: From neuroscience to social science, volume 2* (pp. 207–220). Cambridge, MA: MIT Press.

Dollinger, S. J., & Thelen, M. H. (1978). Leadership and imitation in children. *Personality and Social Psychology Bulletin, 4,* 487–490.

Elgin, C. Z. (1991). Understanding: Art and science. *Midwest Studies in Philosophy, XVI.*

Emerson, R. W. (1841/1982). Self Reliance. In Lazar Ziff (Ed.), *Ralph Waldo Emerson: Selected essays* (pp. 175–203). New York: Penguin.

Emerson, R. W. (1850/1996). *Representative men: Seven lectures.* Cambridge, MA: Harvard University Press.

Erde, E. (1997). On Inadequacy of Role Models for Educating Medical Students in Ethics with Some Reflections on Virtue Theory, *Theoretical Medicine, 18* (1–2) 31–45.

Ervin, S. M. (1964). Language and TAT content in bilinguals. Journal of Abnormal and *Social Psychology, 68,* 500–507.

Evans, M. O. (1992). An estimate of race and gender role-model effects in teaching high school. *Journal of Economic Education, 23* (3), 209–217.

Fireman, G. D., McVay, T. E., Jr., & Flanagan, O. (Eds.) (2003). *Narrative and consciousness: Literature, psychology, and the brain.* New York: Oxford University Press.

Fivush, R. (1991). The social construction of personal narratives. *Merrill-Palmer Quarterly, 37,* 59–82.

Fivush, R. (1994). Constructing narrative, emotion, and self in parent-child conversations about the past. In U. Neisser & R. Fivush (Eds.) *The remembering self: Construction and accuracy in self-narrative* (pp. 136–157). Cambridge: Cambridge University Press.

Fivush, R., & Buckner, J. P. (2003). Creating gender identity through autobiographical narratives. In R. Fivush & C. A. Haden (Eds.), *Autobiographical memory and the construction of a narrative self* (pp. 149–168). Mahwah, NJ: Lawrence Erlbaum. Associates.

Gallagher, S. (2003). Philosophical conceptions of the self: Implications for cognitive science. *Trends in Cognitive Science, 4* (1), 14–21.

Gallese, V., Fadiga, L., Fogassi, L., & Rizzolatti, G. (1996). Action recognition in the premotor cortex. *Brain, 119,* 593–609.

Gallese, V., & Goldman, A. (1998). Mirror neurons and the simulation theory of mind reading. *Trends in Cognitive Sciences, 2* (12), 493–501.

Gattis, M., Bekkering, H., & Wohlschläger, A. (2002). Goal-directed imitation. In A. N. Meltzoff and W. Prinz (Eds.), *The imitative mind: Development, evolution, and brain bases* (pp. 183–205). New York: Cambridge University Press.

Gelley, A. (1995). *Unruly examples—On the rhetoric of exemplarity.* Stanford, CA: Stanford University Press.

Girard, R. (1977). *Violence and the sacred.* Baltimore: John Hopkins University Press.

Glover, J. (1988). *I, the philosophy and psychology of personal identity.* New York: Allen Lane.

Goodman, N. (1997). *Languages of art: An approach to a theory of symbols.* Indianapolis, IN: Hackett. Publishing Company.

Goodman, R. (2002). *Wittgenstein and William James.* Cambridge: Cambridge University Press.

Grèzes, J., & Decety, J. (2001). Functional anatomy of execution, mental simulation, observation, and verb generation of actions: A meta-analysis. *Human Brain Mapping, 12,* 1–19.

Gutmann, A. (1987). *Democratic Education.* Princeton, NJ: Princeton University Press.

Hallie, P. P. (ed.) (1964). *Scepticism, man, & God: Selections from the major writings of Sextus Empiricus.* Middletown: Wesleyan University Press.

Harvey, I. (2002). *Labyrinths of exemplarity.* Albany: State University of New York Press.

Herman, B. (1993). *The practice of moral judgment.* Cambridge, MA: Harvard University Press.

Heyes, C. (2001). Causes and consequences of imitation. *Trends in Cognitive Science, 5* (6), 253–261.

Huesmann, L. (2005). Imitation and the effects of observing media violence on behavior. In S. Hurley & N. Chater (Eds.), *Perspectives on imitation: From neuroscience to social science, volume 2* (pp. 257–266). Cambridge, MA: MIT Press.

Huesmann, L., Eron, L. D., Klein, R., Brice, P., & Fischer, P. (1983). Mitigating the imitation of aggressive behaviors by changing children's attitudes about media violence. *Journal of Personality and Social Psychology, 44* (3), 899–910.

Huesmann, L., Moise, J., Podolski, C., & Eron, L. (2003). Longitudinal relations between childhood exposure to media violence and adult aggression and violence: 1977–1992. *Developmental Psychology, 39,* 201–221.

Hurley, S. (2006). Bypassing conscious control: Media violence, unconscious imitation, and freedom of speech. In S. Pocket, W. Banks, and S. Gallagher (Eds.), *Does consciousness cause behavior? An investigation of the nature of volition (pp. 301-338)*. Cambridge, MA: MIT Press.

Hurley, S., & Chater, N. (Eds.). (2005a). *Perspectives on imitation: From neuroscience to social science, volume 2*. Cambridge, MA: MIT Press.

Hurley, S., & Chater, N. (2005b). Introduction: The Importance of Imitation. In S. Hurley & N. Chater (Eds.), *Perspectives on imitation: From neuroscience to social science, volume 2* (pp. 1–52). Cambridge, MA: MIT Press.

Iacoboni, M., Woods, R. P., Brass, M., Bekkering, H., Mazziotta, J. C., & Rizzolatti, G. (1999). Cortical mechanisms of human imitation. *Science, 286*, 2526–2528.

Jaeger, C. S. (1994). *The envy of angels: Cathedral schools and social ideals in Medieval Europe, 950–1200*. Philadelphia: University of Pennsylvania Press.

James, W. (1890). *Principles of Psychology, volume 2*. New York: Dover.

James, W. (1962). *The writings of William James: A comprehensive edition*. Chicago: University of Chicago Press.

Jastrow, J. (1899). The mind's eye. *Popular Science Monthly, 54*, 299–312.

Johnson, J. G., Cohen, P., Smailes, E. M., Kasen, S., & Brook, J. S. (2002). Television viewing and aggressive behavior during adolescence and adulthood. *Science, 295*, 2468–2471.

Jones, E. E., Jones, R. G., & Gergen, K. J. (1963). Some conditions affecting the evaluation of a conformist. *Journal of Personality, 31*, 270–88.

Kant, I. (1785/ 1993). *Grounding for the metaphysics of morals* (J. Ellington, Trans.). Indianapolis, IN: Hackett.

Kant, I. (1790/19875). *Critique of judgment* (W. Pluhar, Trans.). Indianapolis, IN: Hackett.

Kant, I. (1797/1964). *Doctrine of virtue* (M. J. Gregor, Trans.). New York: Harper and Row.

Kant, I. (1797/1983). Metaphysical principles of virtue (J. W. Ellington, Trans.). In *Immanuel Kant: Ethical philosophy*. Indianapolis, IN: Hackett.

Kauffman, J. M., Hallahan, D. P., Haas, K., Brame, T., & Boren, R. (1978). Imitating children's error to improve spelling performance. *Journal of Learning Disabilities, 11*, 217–222.

Kauffman, J. M, Hallahan, D. P., & Ianna, S. (1977). Suppression of a retardate's tongue protusion by contingent imitation: A case study. *Behavior Research and Therapy, 25*, 196–197.

Kauffman, J. M., Kneedler, R. D., Gamache, R., Hallahan, D. P., & Ball, D. W. (1977). Effects of imitation and nonimitation on children's subsequent behavior. *Journal of Genetic Psychology, 130*, 285–293.

Kauffman, J. M., Snell, M. E. and Hallahan, D. P. (1976). Imitating children during imitation training: two experimental paradigms. *Education and Training in Mental Retardation, 11*, 324–332.

Kelman, H. C. (1961). Processes of opinion change. *The Public Opinion Quarterly, 25* (1), 57-78.

Kierkegaard, S. (1843/1946). Repetition: An essay in experimental psychology. In R. Bretall (ed.), *A Kierkegaard anthology* (pp. 134–152). Princeton, NJ: Princeton University Press.

Kinsbourne, M. (2005). Imitation as entrainment: Brain mechanisms and social consequences. In S. Hurley & N. Chater (Eds.), *Perspectives on imitation: From neuroscience to social science, volume 2* (pp. 163-172). Cambridge, MA: MIT Press.

Klopfenstein, K. (2002). Beyond test scores: The impact of black teacher role models on rigorous math taking. Paper presented at the Western Economic Association International 77th annual conference, Seattle, Washington. Retrieved March 22, 2005, from: http://www.utdallas.edu/research/tsp/pdfpapers/newpaper2.html

Kuhn, T. (1962). *The Structure of scientific revolutions*. Chicago: University of Chicago Press.

Langer, L. L. (2003). The pursuit of death in holocaust narrative. In G. D. Fireman, T. E. McVay, Jr., & O. Flanagan (Eds.), *Narrative and consciousness: Literature, psychology, and the brain.* (pp. 149–165). New York: Oxford University Press.

Lave, J., & Wenger, E. (1991). *Situated learning: Legitimate peripheral participation.* New York: Cambridge University Press.

Leichtman, M. D., Wang, Q., & Pillemer, D. B. (2003). Cultural variations in interdependence and autobiographical memory: Lessons from Korea, China, India, and the United States. In R. Fivush & C.A. Haden (Eds.), *Autobiographical memory and the construction of a narrative self* (pp. 73–98). Mahwah, NJ: Erlbaum.

Lesser, G. S., & Abselson, R. P. (1959). Personality correlates of persuadability in children. In C. L. Hovland & I. L. Janis (Eds.), *Personality and persuadability.* New Haven: Yale University Press.

Lhermitte, F., Pillon, B. and Serdaru, M. (1986). Human autonomy and the frontal lobes: i. Imitation and utilization behavior: a neuropsychological study of 75 patients. *Annals of Neurology, 19*, 326–334.

Liddle, H. G., & Scott, R. (1964). *An intermediate Greek-English lexicon.* Oxford: Oxford University Press.

Link, A. N., & Link J. R. (1999). Women in science: An exploratory analysis of trends in the United States. *Science and Public Policy, 26* (6), 437–442.

Livingston, P. (1992). *Models of desire: Renè Girard and the psychology of mimesis.* Baltimore, MD: Johns Hopkins University Press.

Lloyd Morgan, C. (1896). *Habit and instinct*. London: Arnold.

Locke, J. (1690/1997). *Second treatise on government*. Department of Alfa-informatica, University of Groningen. Retrieved March 20, 1995, from: http://odur.let.rug.nl/~usa/D/1651-1700/locke/ECCG/governxx.htm

Locke, J. (1692/2001). *Some thoughts concerning education*. New York: Bartleby. Retrieved March 15, 2005, from: http://www.bartleby.com/37/1/

Long, A. A., & Sedly, D. N. (1987). *The Hellenistic philosophers, volume 1: Translations of the principle sources with philosophical commentary*. Cambridge: Cambridge University Press.

Louden, R. B. (1992). Go-carts of judgment: Exemplars in Kantian moral education. *Archiv für Geschichte der Philosophie, 74*, 303–22.

Louden, R. B. (1998). Examples in ethics. In E. Craig (Ed.), Routledge encyclopedia of *philosophy*. London: Routledge. Retrieved April 21, 2005, from http://www.rep.routledge.com/article/L023SECT2.

Lucian (1913 version*). Lucian: Volume 1* (A. M. Harmon, trans.). Cambridge, MA: Harvard University Press.

Malherbe, A. J. (1986). *Moral exhortation, a Greco-Roman sourcebook*. Philadelphia: Westminster.

Mandler, J. M., & Johnson N. (1977). Remembrance of things parsed. *Cognitive Psychology, 9*, 111–151.

Marrou, H. I. (1956). *History of education in antiquity*. New York: Mentor.

McDermott, J. J. (1967). Introduction. In *The writings of William James: A comprehensive edition*. Chicago: University of Chicago Press.

Meltzoff, A. N. (2002). Elements of a developmental theory of imitation. In A. N Meltzoff and W. Prinz (Eds.), *The imitative mind: Development, evolution, and brain bases* (pp. 19–41). New York: Cambridge University Press.

Meltzoff, A. N., & Prinz, W. (Eds.) (2002). *The imitative mind: Development, evolution, and brain bases*. New York: Cambridge University Press.

Miller, N. E., & Dollard, J. (1941). *Social learning and imitation*. New Haven: Yale University Press.

Morgan, C. L. (1896). *Habit and instinct*. London: Arnold.

Nadel, J., Guèrini, C., Pezè, A., Rivet, C. (1999). The evolving nature of imitation as a format for communication. In J. Nadel & G. Butterworth (Eds.), *Imitation in infancy* (pp. 209–234). New York: Cambridge University Press.

Nasuti, H. P. (1986). Identity, identification, and imitation: The narrative hermeneutics of Biblical law. *Journal of Law and Religion, 4* (1), 9–23.

Neisser, U., & Fivush, R. (1994). *The remembering self: construction and accuracy in self-narrative*. New York: Cambridge University Press.

Nietzsche, F. (1872/1993). Birth of tragedy. In R. Schacht (Ed.), *Nietzsche: Selections* (pp. 29–40). Englewood Cliffs, NJ: Prentice-Hall.

Nietzsche, F. (1874/1995). Schopenhauer as Educator. In *The complete works of Friedrich Nietzsche, vol. 2: Unfashionable observations* (pp. 171–255). Stanford, CA: Stanford University Press.

Paice, E., Heard, S., & Moss, F. (2002). How important are role models in making good doctors? *British Medical Journal, 325,* 707–710.

Pech, R. J. (2003). Inhibiting imitative terrorism through mimetic engineering. *Journal of Contingencies and Crisis Management, 11* (2), 61–66.

Peters, R. S. (1965). *Education as initiation.* London: Allen & Unwin.

Peters, R. S. (1966). *Ethics and education.* London: Allen & Unwin.

Prinz, W. (2002). Experimental approaches to imitation. In A. N Meltzoff and W. Prinz (Eds.), *The imitative mind: Development, evolution, and brain bases* (pp. 143–162). New York: Cambridge University Press.

Prinz, W., & Meltzoff, A. N. (2002). An introduction to the imitative mind and brain. In A. N. Meltzoff and W. Prinz (Eds.), *The imitative mind: Development, evolution, and brain bases* (pp. 1–15). New York: Cambridge University Press.

Rask, K. N., & Bailey, E. M. (2002). Are faculty role models? Evidence from major choice in an undergraduate institution. *Journal of Economic Education, 33* (2), 99–124.

Rizzolatti, G., Fadiga, L., Fogassi, L., & Gallese, V. (2002). From mirror neurons to imitation: Facts and speculation. In A. N. Meltzoff and W. Prinz (Eds.), *The imitative mind: Development, evolution, and brain bases* (pp. 247–266). New York: Cambridge University Press.

Roberts, M. C. (1980). On being imitated: Effects of levels of imitation and imitator competence. *Social Psychology Quarterly, 43,* 233–240.

Rorty, R. (1989*). Contingency, irony, and solidarity.* Cambridge: Cambridge University Press.

Rosen, S., Musser, L. M., & Brown, J. S. (2002–2003). Reactions of third-graders to recognition allocation after being peer imitated. *Current Psychology: Developmental, Learning, Personality, Social, 21* (4), 319–332.

Rousseau, J. J. (1762/1979). *Emile: Or, on education* (A. Bloom, Trans.). New York: Basic.

Russell, D. A. (1979). De imitatione. In D. West and T. Woodman (Eds.), *Creative imitation and Latin literature.* (pp. 1–16). Cambridge: Cambridge University Press.

Schrauf, R. W., & Rubin, D. C. (2003). On the bilingual's two sets of memories. In R. Fivush & C. A. Haden (Eds.), *Autobiographical memory and the construction of a narrative self* (pp. 121–145). Mahwah, NJ: Erlbaum.

Sinclair, S. (1997). *Making doctors: An institutional apprenticeship.* New York: Oxford International Publishers.

Strawson, G. (2004). Against narrativity. *Ratio, 17* (4), 428-452.

Tan, D. L. (1995). Perceived importance of role models and its relationship with minority student satisfaction and academic performance. *NACADA Journal, 15* (1), 48–51.

Tarde, G. (1903). *The laws of imitation.* New York: Holt.

Thelen, M. H., Frautschi, N. M., Roberts, M. C., Kirkland, K. D., & Dollinger, S. J. (1981). Being imitated, conformity, and social influence: An integrative review. *Journal of Research in Personality, 15,* 403–426.

Thelen, M. H., & Kirkland, K. D. (1976). On status and being imitated: Its effects on attraction and reciprocal imitation. *Journal of Personality and Social Psychology, 33,* 691–697.

Uzgiris, I. C. (1999). Imitation as activity: Its developmental aspects. In J. Nadel & G. Butterworth (Eds.), *Imitation in infancy* (pp. 186–206). New York: Cambridge University Press.

van Baaren, R. B., Holland, R. W., Steenaert, B., van Knippenberg, A. (2003). Mimicry for money: Behavioral consequences of imitation. *Journal of Experimental Social Psychology, 39,* 393–398.

Wilson, J., & Wilson, S. (1998). *Mass media/mass culture: An introduction.* London: McGraw-Hill.

Wittgenstein, L. (1969). *On Certainty* (G. E. M. Amscombe & G. H. Wright, Eds., D. Paul & G. E. M. Amscombe, Trans.). New York: Harper.

Wright, S. M., Kern, D. E., Kolodner, K., Howard, D. M., & Brancati, F.L. (1998). Attributes of excellent attending-physician role models. *New England Journal of Medicine, 339,* 27, 1986–1993.

Zirkel, S. (2002). Is there a place for me? Role models and academic identity among white students and students of color. *Teachers College Record, 104* (2), 357–376.

Index

accordion effect, 8, 34–35, 151n1
action-perception link, 58–61, 122, 139
affirmative action, 67, 142, 149n4
Alcoholics Anonymous, 95
alignment of social markers, 48–49, 141, 144
Annas, Julia, 131
Aristocles, 130
Aristotle, 2, 15, 33–34, 151n4
Arrell, Douglass, 39–41, 148n1
Augustine, Saint, 34

Bandura, Albert, 37–38, 78, 141, 151n2
Bargh, John, 60, 91
Barton, John, 92
Beethoven, Ludwig van, 116
Beyond Good and Evil, 25. *See also* Nietzsche, Friedrich
Bickle, John, 63, 70
Birth of Tragedy, The, 91. *See also* Nietzsche, Friedrich
Broca's area, 70
Bruner, Jerome, 76
Burbules, Nicholas C., 124

Carlyle, Thomas, 1
censorship, 78–81, 144
Cézanne, Paul, 36–37
chameleon effect, 60
charisma, 53–54
Chartrand, Tanya, 60, 91
Chater, Nick, 5

cognitive science, 4–5, 57, 59–61, 68
consequential motivation and imitation. *See under* imitation
Critique of Judgment, 22, 147n5. *See also* Kant, Immanuel
cultural convention, processes of, 39, 141. *See also* exemplification

Decety, Jean, 59
Dennett, Daniel, 62
Derrida, Jacques, 5
Descartes, 19
developmental democracy, 93
Dewey, John, 93
differentiation, process of, 10, 39–51, 128, 140–142, 144. *See also* exemplification
Dijksterhuis, Ap, 62, 144, 149n7
Diogenes Laertius, 130
documentum, 124n3
duck-rabbit drawing, 8, 141

Elgin, Katherine, 35–39, 134
Emerson, Ralph Waldo, 22–24
Emile, 20, 32, 90
emulation, 5–6, 121
Enlightenment, The, 18–26, 89, 109, 139
entrainment, 108
epistemic individualism, 11–12, 19, 26, 109
Erde, Edmund, 110–113, 151n1
examples: communicative nature of, 10, 34–37, 83–108; as community

examples *(continued)*
concern, 45, 48–49, 141; conceptual relationships of, 5; as
constructing ways of seeing and
understanding, 21, 50, 118, 124,
128, 135–136, 148n7; critical
engagement with, 12, 109–138,
143; as different from surrounding context, 39–51; educational
aims and, 31, 129–137; educational institutions and, 50, 141–
145; evaluating for coherence,
132–134, 137–138, 142; genius and,
22; as human models for imitation, 13–18, 82, 127–138; induction
and, 33–34; as inspiration, 21, 24–
25, 118, 147n6; intentional
selection of, 28, 31–32, 37, 122,
128; as invitations to community,
97–100, 118, 124–125, 147n2; as
normative patterns or models, 33,
50–51, 53–54; as opposed to
autonomy, 21, 119–120; as parts of
wholes, 33; as posing questions,
23–24, 118; practices and, 134–136;
as reminders of ideals, 21, 23–25;
as revealing future selves, 32, 43,
50, 140, 143; rotation and, 134–
136, 138; social nature of, 10, 25,
29, 36–37, 43–44, 48–50, 128, 137,
139–145; as sources of information, 18, 121. *See also* exemplification; role models; teaching
strategies; practical objection to
imitating examples; theoretical
objection to imitating examples
exemplars. *See* examples
exemplification: conceptually related
to imitation, 6–9; created by
context, 39–44,
128, 139–145; critical thinking and,
12, 49, 109–125, 129–138; democracy and, 48–49, 144–145; insufficiency of evaluative beliefs in,
44–45; insufficiency of exaggerat-

ing a trait in, 37–38, 41–42;
insufficiency of possessing a trait
in, 34–37, 142; involved with
perception, 7–9; processes that
determine, 10, 37–44, 128, 140–
144; questions about, 32–33. *See
also* examples; differentiation,
process of; cultural convention,
process of

fabric sample example, 35, 37
Fivush, Robyn, 63, 74, 76, 80
Freud, Sigmund, 56

Gallagher, Shaun, 149n3
Gallese, Vittorio, 59, 68
Gandhi, Mahatma, 36
Gelley, Alexander, 33, 147n5
Girard, René, 97, 106, 149n1
Globe Program, 107, 151n9
Glover, Jonathan, 75
Goldman, Alvin, 59, 68
Goodman, Nelson, 5, 35–37
Goodman, Russell, 123–124, 151n5
*Grounding for the Metaphysics of
Morals*, 119. *See also* Kant,
Immanuel

Harvey, Irene, 5, 21, 32, 49, 128
Herman, Barbara, 147n4
Heyes, Cecilia, 149n2
History of Rome, 15
Homer, 10, 13–15, 130
Hurley, Susan, 5, 149n6

identification theory, 56, 150n3
ideomotor action, 57, 142. *See also*
action-perception link
Illiad, 14, 129. *See also* Homer
imitation: behaviorist account of, 55–
56; as betrayal of reason and
authenticity, 19–25, 28–29, 110–113,
119–120; in the Bible, 92–93, 147n2;
as commendation, 87–89, 94, 107;
communicative function of, 84–93;

as communion with God, 92; conceptual relationship to exemplification, 6–9; consequential motivation and, 27–28, 54–57, 73, 121; creativity and, 22, 108, 109–125, 151n2; critical reason and, 10–12, 16, 28–29, 67, 108, 109–138, 143; education and, 11, 78–81, 85–86, 97–100, 105–107, 114, 119, 136–138; enabling conditions and, 67–69, 149n5; in Enlightenment education, 18–26; factors influencing meaning of, 101–105; in Greco-Roman education, 13–17, 22, 25–26, 90, 109; of God, 2, 84, 92; human freedom and, 16, 21–22; infants and, 59–60, 68, 72, 86; initiation and, 97–100; as instinctual response, 55, 148n8; in Latin literature, 104, 117; meanings of, 84–108, 139, 150n6–7; as mediating community, 93–108, 139; in medieval education, 17–18, 26; as mockery, 87–89; narrative-self theory of, 65–82, 142–144; neuroscience and, 59–60; process-oriented type of, 105–107, 114–116, 143; promoting self-knowledge, 90–92; psychoanalytic account of, 56–57, 149n1; result-oriented type of, 105–106, 114–116, 143; role of motivation in, 10, 57–61; self as sorting mechanism for, 61–62; as sign of openness, 91; social meanings of, 11, 83–107; social nature of, 73–77, 83–108, 113–119, 139–145; of students, 87, 107; technical definition of, 5–6; as theodicy, 91; as tool for influence, 88–89. *See also* mimesis; practical objection to imitating examples; theoretical objection to imitating examples
Impressionism, 114
intentional selection of examples. *See under* examples
Isocrates, 15–16, 85–86, 88, 147n7

Jaeger, Stephen C., 17, 147n3
James, William, 57–61, 66, 70–71, 77, 123–124, 128, 142

Kant, Immanuel, 21–22, 24–25, 119–120, 147n4–5
Kelman, Herbert, 150n3
Kierkegaard, Søren, 83–84
Kinsbourne, Marcel, 107–108
Kuhn, Thomas, 133

Langer, Lawrence, 63
language, 73–74
Languages of Art, 35
Lave, Jean, 95
Livingston, Paisley, 149n1, 150n5
Livy, 15
Lloyd Morgan, Conwy, 55, 148n8
Locke, John, 2, 17–18, 19, 103, 105
Lucian of Samosata, 16, 46–48, 148n3

McDermott, John, 118
media violence, 4, 36, 50, 78–81, 143–145, 149n6–7
medical education, 3–4, 50, 111–112, 140–143
Meltzoff, Andrew, 59–60, 68, 72, 149n2
mimesis, 85, 97
mimetic engineering, 148n2
mimicry, 5–6, 89, 91. *See also* imitation
mirror neurons, 59, 68, 70
moral education, 11, 90, 92, 109–126, 131
Moralia, 91
Moralium dogma philosophorum, 17

Nadel, Jacqueline, 84, 86
narrative self, 62–65, 73–77, 80–81
narrative-self theory of imitation. *See under* imitation
negative congruence, 65–67, 70
negative examples, 4, 7, 11, 15, 32, 50, 54, 72, 78–79, 134–144

neutral congruence, 65–67, 70
Nietzsche, Friedrich, 2, 10, 91, 120

Odyssey, 14. *See also* Homer
On Certainty, 123; Wittgenstein, Ludwig
ownership of action, 103–107

Parallel Lives of Greeks and Romans, 45. *See also* Plutarch
Pech, Richard J., 148n2
people-oriented physicians, 3, 140–143. *See also* medical education
Peters, R.S., 97
Phaedrus, 15. *See also* Plato
plagiarism, 100, 103–105
Plato, 2, 15, 24, 33, 130, 137
Plutarch, 15, 45–49, 91–92, 144, 148n7
Pollock, Jackson, 35, 39–40
positive congruence, 65–67, 70
practical objection to imitating examples, 109–119
pragmatism, 123, 133–134, 151n3
priming effect, 60
Princip, Gavrilo, 7, 34, 50, 131, 151n1
Principles of Psychology, 58–59, 123. *See also* James, William
Prinz, Wolfgang, 59–61
Pyrrho of Elis, 12, 129–131. *See also* Skeptics

reason, nature of, 122–125, 128
repetition, meaning of, 83–84
Representative Men, 23. *See also* Emerson, Ralph Waldo
response priming, 6
Rhetoric, 33. *See also* Aristotle
role models, 2, 3, 12, 67, 110–113, 139–140, 142–143
Rorty, Richard, 133
Rousseau, Jean-Jacques, 2, 5, 19–23, 25, 32, 90
Russell, D. A., 104, 117

scientific communities, 105–107, 113
Second Treatise of Government, 103. *See also* Locke, John
self-imitation, 20
Self Reliance, 22. *See also* Emerson, Ralph Waldo
Sextus Empiricus, 134–135. *See also* Skeptics
Skeptics, 2, 12, 129–138
Smeyers, Paul, 124
Social Learning and Imitation, 55
social learning theory, 15, 55
Socrates, 15, 115, 127, 130, 137
Some Thoughts Concerning Education, 17–18, 19. *See also* Locke, John
standard model: continued usefulness of, 78, 81, 121; elements of, 15, 26; premodern examples of, 13–18; problematic assumptions of, 10, 26–29, 31, 54–55, 70, 122, 128, 139
status-oriented physicians, 3, 140–143. *See also* medical education
stimulus enhancement, 6
storytelling conventions, 74–76, 80–81, 95
storytelling skills, 76–77, 80–81
Strawson, Galen, 63–65

Tarde, Gabriel de, 55
teaching strategies, 14, 26–28, 31–32, 44–50, 128, 136–138, 140–145
temporal mediation of community: future goals and, 96–97; implications for education of, 97–100, 105–107; past understandings and, 94–95; present boundary markers and, 95–96; as response to the practical objection, 113–114
Thelen, Mark, 87–89, 150n2, 150n6
theoretical objection to imitating examples, 109, 119–125
Timon of Phlius, 129–131
tutelary beliefs, 32, 44–45
To Phillip, 16, 147n6

utilitarianism, 120
Uzgiris, Ina C., 86

vicarious reinforcement, 15, 78
violence, 97. *See also* media violence
Violence and the Sacred, 97
virtue, 90–92

voluntary action, 58, 60–61
von Zirclaere, Thomasin, 17

Wenger, Etienne, 95
will. *See* voluntary action
Wittgenstein, Ludwig, 2, 123–124,
    128